The Criminal Justice Report Writing Guide for Officers

Jean Reynolds, Ph.D.
Polk State College
Winter Haven, Florida

The Maple Leaf Press

www.YourPoliceWrite.com

Printed in the USA

Copyright © 2011 Jean Reynolds

Introduction

Effective report writing is vital to your criminal-justice career. Your reports are public documents that may be read by supervisors, attorneys, judges, citizens, and reporters. Quality reports impress superiors, win respect from colleagues, and help bring offenders to justice. They facilitate investigations and provide statistics that help shape hiring decisions, budget proposals, and policy changes.

If you work for a community agency, your reports will help you prepare for jury trials—and may even prevent cases from ending up in court. Defense attorneys who read your reports hoping to find omissions and errors may decide not to try for an acquittal after all.

In a correctional institution, your reports are the instruments that begin the disciplinary process. Inmates who experience the consequences of their behavior are more likely to conform to society's standards at the end of their sentences.

Your writing skills can help you advance in your career. You'll be prepared to communicate effectively with the media, community leaders, and government officials. Well-written reports help you create a reputation for professionalism, accuracy, and fairness that will stand you in good stead as you start to climb the career ladder.

This book offers you a wealth of information about report writing. A pretest will help you assess your strengths and determine which skills need your attention. Section I shows you how to organize and write professional reports. Sections II and III cover sentence skills, Section IV help you avoid usage errors, and Section V covers special words you need to know. A post-test helps you decide what areas need further review. Exercises are provided throughout the book, and an Answer Key allows you to check your progress at each step. Let's get started!

Resources for Instructors, Academies, and Agencies

A supplemental booklet containing printable exercises and an Answer Key for Chapters 1 – 12 is available free to authorized users. Send an email from your agency, school, or institution to jreynoldswrite@aol.com. You can also download instructional PowerPoints for the first 12 chapters at www.YourPoliceWrite.com. No registration or request is necessary.

Acknowledgments

First I want to thank everyone from the Kenneth C. Thompson Institute of Public Safety who helped me learn about criminal justice and report writing: Charles E. Pottinger, the late Mary Mariani, and Don Shattler.

Cheryl Day from Polk State College helped me with word-processing issues. Dr. David Kuehl and William Fienga made valuable suggestions. Gretchen Baut from Zoemedia helped with the publishing process and created the supplemental website, www.YourPoliceWrite.com. And, as always, I thank my husband, Charles Reynolds, for his love and support.

PRETEST

Instructions: Complete each activity below. When you're finished, check your responses against the Pretest Answer Key beginning on page 8.

Part I Effective Reports

Instructions: Put a check √ if a sentence meets the requirements for an effective report. Put an X if the sentence does not meet the requirements.

_____1. I smelled alcohol on Lennon's breath.

_____2. Inmate Johnson was belligerent when I entered his cell.

_____3. I looked through the open front door and saw a man with both his hands around a woman's neck.

_____4. Carol Todd was watching television while I questioned her husband.

_____5. I saw Fowler's car cross the double line three times as he drove down Second Street.

_____6. It was obvious that Fowler's driving was impaired, probably by alcohol.

_____7. After looking for the point of entry, I asked Barker which items were missing from his apartment.

_____8. Inmate Powers refused to cooperate.

Part II Effective Word Choices

Instructions: Put a check √ if the wording of the sentence meets the requirements for a modern report. Put an X if it does not.

____1. Sarah Wilson advised me that she had left for work at 7:45 that morning.

____2. A small plastic bag of white powder was found when Inmate Clem Johnson's cell was searched by this officer.

____3. I ascertained that Buckley had taken Hill's watch during the scuffle.

____4. I asked Anderson if she needed medical help, and she nodded her head up and down.

____5. Sawyer cursed and swore when he saw the handcuffs.

____6. I processed the area while Officer Gage questioned Lillian Thompson.

____7. The window over the kitchen sink was broken, and pieces of glass were lying on the kitchen counter.

____8. When I contacted Jeffrey Klein, the neighbor, he denied having seen or heard anything unusual.

Part III English Usage

Instructions: Put a check √ in front of any sentence that meets the requirements for English usage. Put an X in front of any sentence that does not meet the requirements.

____1. Paula Dillon gave permission for my partner and I to search the basement.

____2. The Quinns have lived in the house on Central Boulevard for two years.

____3. The women's descriptions of their attacker were detailed and consistent.

_____4. There's records of two previous calls about suspicious behavior at that address.

_____5. Felicia Jones told me that her Father had been gone all weekend.

_____6. Inmate Perkins told me that "I wouldn't find anything in his locker and should leave him alone."

_____7. The cut looked serious, it obviously needed medical attention.

_____8. The neighbor whom I interviewed gave me a description of the suspect.

PRETEST ANSWER KEY

Page numbers refer to sections of this book with information about the skills on this test.

Part I Effective Reports

X 1. I smelled alcohol on Lennon's breath. [Alcohol is odorless. You should say that you smelled an alcoholic beverage or liquor.]

X 2. Inmate Johnson was belligerent when I entered his cell. [Page 49: Vague. State exactly what Johnson said or did.]

√ 3. I looked through the open front door and saw a man with both his hands around a woman's neck.

√ 4. Carol Sanders was watching television while I questioned her husband.

√ 5. I saw Fowler's car cross the double line three times as he drove down Second Street.

X 6. It was obvious that Fowler's driving was impaired, probably by alcohol. [Page 49: This kind of statement may not fare well in a courtroom. State what you saw Fowler do, and omit your opinion.]

X 7. After looking for the point of entry, I asked Barker which items were missing from his apartment.

X 8. Inmate Powers refused to cooperate. [Page 49: Vague. State exactly what Powers said or did.]

Part II Effective Word Choices

X 1. Sarah Wilson advised me that she had left for work at 7:45 that morning. [Page 169: Sarah Wilson *told* you she had left for work. Save "advise" for actual advice.]

X 2. A small plastic bag of white powder was found when Inmate Clem Johnson's cell was searched by this officer. [Page 71: Avoid passive voice. A better sentence would be: "I found a small plastic bag of white powder when I searched Inmate Clem Johnson's cell." See page 51 for more about using "I" and "me" instead of the outdated phrase "this officer."]

X 3. I ascertained that Buckley had taken Hill's watch during the scuffle. [Page 169: Ascertained" is police jargon that should be avoided. Another problem: This sentence doesn't explain how you know what Buckley had done.]

√ 4. I asked Anderson if she needed medical help, and she nodded her head up and down.

X 5. Sawyer cursed and swore when he saw the handcuffs. [Page 175: *Curse* means to call down evil powers; *swear* means taking an oath. And you should write exactly what Sawyer said, word-for-word, instead of generalizing: See page 27.]

X 6. I processed the area while Officer Gage questioned Lillian Thompson. [Pages 56 and 169: *Processed* is vague: What did you look for, and what did you find?]

√ 7. The window over the kitchen sink was broken, and pieces of glass were lying on the kitchen counter.

X 8. When I contacted Jeffrey Klein, the neighbor, he denied having seen or heard anything unusual. [Page 168: *Contacted* is vague: Did you phone, visit, or email Klein?]

Part III English Usage

X 1. Paula Dillon gave permission for my partner and I to search the basement. [Page 129: *my partner and me*]

√ 2. The Quinns have lived in the house on Central Boulevard for two years.

√ 3. The women's descriptions of their attacker were detailed and consistent.

X 4. There's records of two previous calls about suspicious behavior at that address. [Page 137: *There are records*]

X 5. Felicia Jones told me that her Father had been gone all weekend. [Page 142: Lower-case *father*]

X 6. Inmate Perkins told me that "I wouldn't find anything in his locker and should leave him alone." [Page 125: Not Perkins' exact words, so delete the quotation marks.]

X 7. The cut looked serious, it obviously needed medical attention. [Page 86: There are two sentences; change the comma to a period, and capitalize *it*.]

√ 8. The neighbor whom I interviewed gave me a description of the suspect.

Section I: Writing the Report

Chapter 1

Why Is Report Writing Important?

Think back to when you first decided on a criminal justice career. What attracted you? Chances are it *wasn't* report writing. Officers frequently say that writing is *not* a favorite task: It's time consuming, tiring, and exacting—and there are serious consequences if they make a mistake.

But report writing is essential to your career as a police or corrections officer, and writing becomes even more important as you advance up the career ladder. In fact it can even help your superiors decide that you're qualified for promotions and greater responsibility.

Your reports play a vital role in the day-to-day functioning of an agency or institution. First, they attest to your professionalism. In addition, the facts and actions in your reports may be used to:

- provide data for statistical studies
- help justify an arrest or disciplinary action
- testify that you are following legal guidelines
- provide vital clues for follow-up investigation

Who Reads Reports?

Many people both inside and outside the criminal justice system may read the reports you write, drawing conclusions about the choices you made when you dealt with a particular situation.

A well-written report can impress a supervisor, newspaper reporter, or defense attorney. It might be the deciding factor when a district attorney decides whether to proceed with a prosecution. Family members, community leaders, researchers, and government officials are all potential readers of your reports. It stands to reason, then, that you need to make an extra effort to write accurate, complete, and grammatical reports.

What Goes into a Good Report?

Report writing can sound intimidating if you're new to the criminal justice field. It's important to know, however, that several factors are already working to your advantage. First, you're already a writer. The writing skills you learned in school will give you a good foundation to build on as you learn about report writing.

Second, help is available if you need to brush up on grammar and usage. Here's a summary of the skills you need to write effective sentences, paragraphs, and reports:

- three comma rules (page 105)
- two ways to use apostrophes (page 121)
- four pronoun rules (page 127)
- five rules for capital letters (page 141)
- six subject-verb agreement rules (page 137)

In addition, you need to master criminal-justice vocabulary (page 167), and you need to watch for some commonly misused words (your/you're, to/too, break/brake, and others—see pages 173-82).

And here's a tip: The chapters about Avoiding Common Errors (page 153) and Myths about Grammar (page 159) are short and readable, and they can teach you a lot about writing in a short time.

All these skills are covered in this book, and practice exercises and answers are included. You can also ask family members, friends, and co-workers to look at your writing and help you spot problem sentences. Take note: With practice, *every officer* can become a competent writer.

Third—and this is perhaps the best news—report writing is predictable, even though police and corrections work is not. Most reports fall into four types. Learn the special requirements for each type, and you're assured of producing an effective report every time you sit down to write.

The bottom line is that professional writing skills are within reach of *any officer*—including you—provided, of course, that you're willing to invest the time and energy needed to be an effective writer.

Exercise 1 Why Are Reports Important?

Instructions: Imagine that a friend has been talking with you about a possible career in criminal justice. He or she is looking forward to the excitement of police or corrections work. Your friend disliked English in high school and hopes to spend as little time as possible writing reports on the job.

Write a short letter explaining why report writing is important and offering suggestions for sharpening the skills needed. When you're finished, check your ideas against the list on page 191 in the Answer Key.

Chapter 2

Overview of Report Writing

Report formats vary from agency to agency, and from institution to institution. Some officers write their reports on blank sheets of paper, while others use paper forms or computer templates with boxes and bubbles ready to fill in. But *all* reports share some common features, and all require the same qualities:

- accuracy, brevity, and completeness
- objectivity
- a step-by-step account of the events that occurred
- details about the people and places involved

Although details may vary, depending on the agency or institution you're working for and the kind of situation you're dealing with, the basic features of a report are always the same. You begin by establishing the day and time, location, people involved, and type of incident.

What follows is a narrative (story) of what happened. There may also be witnesses, evidence, and an investigation. Finally you will wrap up your report with a conclusion: What charges were filed (if any), where evidence is stored (if any), whether medical personnel were called to the scene, and so on.

By now you're probably thinking—correctly—that you already know much of what's needed to write an effective report. You observe, ask questions, and write the information down accurately. You think about each category: What you saw, and what the outcome was. Congratulations! You're well on your way to writing effective reports.

Sample Reports

Let's examine two reports—one for a police department, and one for a correctional institution—to see how they're organized.

Report for a Police Department

This report was written by Officer Carole Donner when she was dispatched to a break-in.

At 3:20 p.m. on October 3, 2010, I, Officer Carole Donner, was dispatched to a break-in at 35 Woodland Road.

I talked to Sam Farley (DOB 03/11/1961), the homeowner. He told me that he had been shopping at Wal-Mart. When he arrived home at approximately 3:00 p.m., he saw the front door was slightly open. He got out his cell phone and called 911.

I went into the house and saw and heard no one. In the living room I saw an empty space on a TV stand. Mr. Farley showed me what he said was the master bedroom. A chest of drawers was against the west wall with three drawers on the floor in front of it. There were three empty spaces in the dresser. I saw clothing, men's underwear, men's shirts, and other cloth items on the floor and in the dresser drawers.

Farley told me that his SONY Bravia 32" TV (serial number RB1534780) was missing. Also missing was a Rolex watch, a diamond ring, and approximately $225 in cash that he had put into the top dresser drawer in the master bedroom. Farley said he had photographs of the watch and ring stored in a safe deposit box at First National Bank. He promised to bring the photos to the station on Monday afternoon.

I took fingerprints from the front door, the TV stand, and the chest of drawers. I checked the windows and rear door. There were no signs of tampering.

I interviewed a neighbor, Alisa Cole (DOB 07/15/1949), in the house to the right, at 31 Woodland Road. She said she had been watching TV that afternoon. She heard a car pull into Farley's driveway sometime after 2 p.m. She had assumed it was Farley and did not get up to look. She did not hear the car pull away.

I signed the fingerprints over to the officer in charge of the evidence room. I told Farley that a detective would be in touch with him.

Report for a Correctional Institution

This report was written by correctional officer Frank Dunham.

At 10:35 a.m. on July 9, 2010, I, Officer Frank Dunham, went into Building B to talk to the chaplain about plans for next month's musical program.

As I opened the door to the chaplain's office, I heard footsteps behind me. I turned and saw Inmate James Harper DC 091724 exiting the storage closet.

When he saw me, he put his hands behind his back. I told him to stop and show me what was in his hands. He said, "Don't go telling me what to do, man."

I again ordered Harper to show me what was in his hands. He turned around, and I saw three ballpoint pens in each hand. I checked his pockets and found two rolls of transparent tape.

I confiscated the pens and tape and escorted Inmate Harper to Disciplinary Confinement. I returned to Building B and reminded the chaplain about department regulations requiring the storage closet to be locked at all times.

A Closer Look

Take a moment to reread these two reports. Then list the features the reports have in common. When you're finished, compare your list to the list below.

Here are some of the features you might have noticed:

- The reports have a beginning, middle, and end
- Both officers explained why they were at the scene
- The date, time, and place were recorded, along with names of persons they talked to
- The officers recorded what they saw and did, along with what they were told

- The reports ended with a wrap-up explaining the outcome of the situation

You might also have noticed that the officers used "I" and "me" when referring to themselves. They wrote clear, simple sentences, and they stuck to the facts, avoiding opinions and guesses about what had happened.

The Stages of Report Writing

Like any writing task, report writing proceeds in three stages: Preparation, drafting, and revising.

Preparation includes observing, interviewing, investigating, and taking notes.

Drafting involves organizing and recording the information on paper or a laptop. You may be given a paper form with spaces for names, date, location, offense, and other information. If you're using a laptop, you'll be typing this information into spaces on the screen.

Revising includes spellchecking, verifying information, and checking for correct English usage, clarity, completeness, and professional style.

This book will offer you tips for effectively completing every step in the report-writing process.

Meeting the Challenge

Officers new to the criminal justice field sometimes underestimate the sophisticated thinking skills required for effective report writing. As you write your report, you may need to:

- blend two sets of stories—what happened before you arrived at the scene, and what you observed yourself

- accurately recall and record what witnesses and suspects tell you
- sift through conflicting accounts to determine what really happened
- select the information needed for follow-up investigation, if necessary
- eliminate bias and emotion from your account
- justify your actions
- build a strong case for prosecution and conviction

Here are some important points to remember when you write a report:

1. Use names.

Avoid labels like "victim" or "suspect," which quickly become confusing. Give the person's full name the first time, and then switch to last names only. If two or more people have the same last name, you can use their first names. Don't use "Mr." and "Mrs.": Once you've established the family name as "Johnson," you can refer to the spouses by their first names.

2. Be efficient.

Don't write "month of September": September is always a month. Don't write "for the purpose of" when you mean "for" or "to." You can see a list of time-wasting words and expressions beginning on page 167.

3. Don't write statements that might be challenged.

Avoid hunches, guesses, and predictions. Don't say, for example, that a suspect *attempted*, *tried*, *intended*, or *planned* to do a particular action. Write only what you've seen or heard: You saw the suspect climb a tree, break a window, and enter the house. (See page 49 to learn more.)

4. Be complete. If you gave a sobriety test or looked for fingerprints, include the results, even if they were negative. If you took evidence away from the scene, list each item and explain what happened to it ("chain of custody"). If you called for an ambulance or provided a victim's brochure, note those actions in your report.

5. Don't generalize.

Words like *upset, enraged, scared, nervous,* and *disturbed* are too vague for a criminal justice report and can cause problems for you in a courtroom. Describe exactly what you saw or heard: Shaking hands, darting eyes, clenched fists.

Other vague words to avoid are *weapon* (Smith-Wesson revolver? shotgun? X-Acto knife? baseball bat?), *contacted* (phoned? visited? emailed?), and *noticed* (heard? saw?).

6. Be prepared to describe some of the physical details of a scene.

Practice ahead of time so that you can easily identify north, south, east, and west in any area in your agency's jurisdiction or your correctional institution. Know the length of your stride so that you can estimate lengths and distances. Train yourself to notice height, eye color, skin color, clothing, and distinctive characteristics: facial hair, tattoos, eyeglasses, and jewelry. If your cell phone has a camera feature, learn how to use it.

7. Write like the professional you are.

If you're writing on a computer, use the spellchecker and grammar checker. These electronic tools are not foolproof, but they will catch many errors. Make a list of words that you have difficulty spelling, and make sure it's handy whenever you write a report. Whenever possible, have someone read over your reports before you submit them to a supervisor.

Exercise 2 Rewrite a Paragraph

Instructions: A paragraph from a police report is printed below. Using what you have learned, evaluate the paragraph. (Do not be concerned about the parts of the report that have been omitted.) When you're finished, go to page 191 to check your answers.

...Victim 1 [Ted Wilkins, DOB 8/13/75] seemed upset. I didn't think I'd get any useful information from him, so I began to interview Victim 2 (Geena Wilkins, wife, DOB 5/10/77]. She was calmer and described the intruder. She said he was about 5' 10", white, with brown eyes and brown hair. He had no facial hair. He was wearing dark-blue jeans, a red plaid shirt, and white lace-up shoes. She seemed intelligent when I was talking to her, so I figured she was probably accurate. I checked the door for signs of forced entry, and then I checked to see if the windows were locked....

Chapter 3

Preparing to Write

A good report begins before you start writing. As you're observing, interviewing, and taking notes, you need to make an extra effort to ensure that you have all the facts needed for a complete report. Here are some important guidelines:

1. Be prepared to take notes.

Of course you have writing paper (and perhaps a laptop). But what if you jump out of your patrol car to deal with an emergency? It's embarrassing to be caught without writing materials. Go to the Dollar Store and buy a few tiny notebooks. Keep one in a pocket, along with a couple of pens, just in case you need it. (A reminder: If you keep your notes, they're subject to subpoena. Don't mix personal information with your job-related notes.)

2. Think about categories.

Train yourself to think in six categories: **yourself**, **victims**, **witnesses**, **suspects**, **evidence**, and **disposition**. You won't necessarily organize your report in these categories. But thinking about them will ensure that you don't overlook anything important. (You'll learn more about these categories beginning on page 31.)

3. Think about the type of report you'll be rewriting.

If you've thoroughly familiarized yourself with the types of reports and their special requirements, you're more likely to cover every angle. For example, a Type 4 report (officer sets the case in motion) may have to deal with probable cause issues in some detail. You can learn more about types of reports beginning on page 39.

4. Train yourself to observe and remember.

Make an extra effort to look, listen, and remember, especially when you first arrive at a potential crime scene. Look for skid marks, broken shrubbery, and shattered glass. Listen for voices, and be able to label them: a man? a woman? a child? Is furniture tipped over? Do you smell alcoholic beverages? Look for blood and injuries, and be prepared to describe what you observed in detail.

5. Record information promptly and thoroughly.

Don't rely on your memory to add details lately. It's embarrassing to be caught with an inaccurate or incomplete report. Discipline yourself to write a complete set of notes as soon as possible.

This completeness requirement may sound easy: Just write down everything that happened, right?

Unfortunately, it's not that simple. Officers often forget to record a piece of essential information. For example, an officer might mention a sobriety test but forget to record the results. Or an officer will forget to note that she wasn't the one who interviewed a witness: It was her partner. Problems can arise later on when an investigation stalls or a court hearing has to be postponed because important facts are missing.

Interviews

Talking to witnesses, suspects, and victims can present challenges: Stress levels are likely to be high, and you may be listening to a jumble of relevant and irrelevant information. Sorting everything out and accurately recording what you heard can be a complex and time-consuming task.

1. Deal with emotions first. Reassure the person you're talking to ("You're safe" or "We've got the situation under control"). Then explain that you need the person's help in order to follow up.

26

When you're calm and professional, the person who's talking is more likely to cooperate and answer your questions. Don't hesitate to break in, gently, if a witness goes off on a tangent.

2. Provide as much privacy as you can during the interview. Witnesses may be more forthcoming when they're not observed, especially if the suspect is at the scene.

3. Remember that hearsay is permissible in criminal justice reports—and it can provide valuable clues for investigators.

Some perpetrators have a consistent, repetitive pattern of words and actions. So go ahead and record what a witness heard and saw, even though you're getting the information secondhand.

4. Use quotation marks in your notes any time you write down a witness or suspect's exact words. That information may be useful in a court hearing later on.

5. Don't rely on your memory. You can't always predict how much time will pass before you get a chance to write up your notes as a formal report.

6. Record slang and bad language, even if it sounds unprofessional. Knowing a suspect's exact words may be useful in an investigation or court hearing later on, for example. Be sure to ask for explanations if a witness or suspect uses unusual slang or vague language. Children, too, may have difficulty finding the right word.

Completeness

Here are some tips to ensure your report is complete:

1. Make an extra effort to get contact information from anyone who might assist in an investigation, especially in a major case. If you

suspect you might have difficulty reaching a victim or witness, ask for a backup telephone number for a friend or family member.

2. Always include the results of an investigation, even if the results were negative.

Sometimes the absence of evidence can be as important as something you find. Suppose, for example, someone returns to the scene later to plant evidence there that might incriminate an innocent person. Your written statement that the weapon (or fingerprints or bloodstains) weren't there when you did your investigation can change the outcome of the case.

Here are some examples of things you might look for that should be documented in your report, no matter what results you get:

- point of entry or exit
- missing or damaged items
- vehicular damage
- signs of trauma
- signs of substance abuse
- evidence of a break-in
- fingerprints
- results of a sobriety test
- evidence of vehicular damage
- blood and other bodily fluids

3. Be particularly careful to document evidence that establishes probable cause, especially in Type 4 situations when you, the officer, set the case in motion–a traffic stop, for example. Even a strong case against a suspect can be thrown out of court if you can't establish a solid reason for getting involved.

4. Remember to document any steps you've taken to protect a crime scene, such as marking the area with crime tape or posting an officer to screen visitors.

5. Be sure to establish a chain of custody for evidence. What items did you remove from the scene, and what actions (tag, package, mark, sketch, log) did you take?

Exercise 3 Preparing to Write

Instructions: Choose the correct answer to each question below. When you're finished, check your answers on page 192.

1. Dealing with a victim's emotions
   a) is not part of an officer's job
   b) should usually be the first step in an interview
   c) should be done only after all the facts are recorded
   d) is rarely necessary

2. "Chain of custody"
   a) refers to transporting a suspect
   b) refers to filing a report
   c) refers to evidence taken at the scene
   d) does not need to be recorded in a report

3. Having extra paper and pens in a pocket
   a) may be helpful in an emergency
   b) is unprofessional
   c) violates most agency's regulations
   d) may damage an officer's uniform

4. Which of the following does *not* need to be documented in a report?
   a) results of a sobriety test
   b) vehicular damage

    c) point of entry

    d) the officer's theories about how and why the crime was committed

5. Slang

    a) has no place in a report

    b) may require a definition if it's unfamiliar

    c) should be used only if it's grammatical

    d) should be used only if it's easily understood

Chapter 4

Organizing a Report

By their very nature, police and correctional reports are challenging to organize. A good report is actually a combination of many groups of information. Much of the report will be a simple narrative (story), listing in order the events that happened. But reports may contain flashbacks, and many have contradictory statements from witnesses and suspects who have different versions of what happened. Even experienced officers say that organizing all this information can be difficult.

As suggested on page 25, you can simplify the organizing process by training yourself to think in six broad categories: **yourself**, **victims**, **witnesses**, **suspects**, **evidence**, and **disposition**. Of course these categories are too general to be applied to every situation. Sometimes they'll even overlap. But they will always help you organize your reports, and they can be adapted to almost everything you write.

You should start mentally organizing your report at the scene, while you're recording facts in your notebook. If you're thinking about specific categories, your notes are likely to be clear and complete, and your report will be easier to write.

Reminder: These headings are *thinking tools:* You won't use them in your actual report.

The **first category** covers everything done by **you** (and your partner, if present). How did you get involved? Were you dispatched, or did you observe something suspicious? Later you will use this category to establish probable cause.

Sometimes you will need more than one paragraph to describe your actions. In a domestic dispute, for example, your first paragraph might describe what you saw when you entered the house. A later paragraph could tell what happened after you arrived.

In a correctional institution, staff members are often the sole witnesses to the disciplinary problems that are written up in reports. Because your observations may be the only proof that a rule was violated, accuracy and thoroughness are essential.

The **second category** includes statements made by the **victims** you've questioned. This is a good place for the background information that led to the crime. Usually you will need a separate paragraph for each victim's statement.

The **third category** covers statements made by **witnesses**, with a separate paragraph for each. This category is another appropriate place for background information.

The **fourth category** covers statements, descriptions, and actions of **suspects**. Suspects may give information that conflicts with what victims and witnesses tell you. Be sure to make an accurate and objective record of everything you're told.

With the **fifth category**, **evidence**, the focus returns to you, the officer. Using your professional knowledge, describe your investigation. Information may include entry and exit points, injuries, fingerprints, weapons, torn clothing, damage to property, and other physical evidence.

The **sixth category**, **disposition**, documents the immediate outcome. Did you call for an ambulance, take fingerprints, make an arrest, read from your Miranda card, offer a victims' brochure? Were weapons seized? Will you be turning any evidence over to the department? If you gave sobriety tests, what were the results?

Chapter 5

Writing a Report

Now it's time to expand the information in your notes into complete sentences and paragraphs.

If you're using a department-issued laptop or a paper form provided by your agency, you'll begin by filling in the spaces with information from your notes. Your actual writing process will begin when you come to the space used for your narrative.

If you're writing your report on a blank piece of paper, you'll begin your report with an opening sentence that serves two functions. First, it answers the "5W" questions: **who**, **what**, **when**, **where**, **why**. Second, it establishes **probable cause**. If you can't justify why you became involved in the situation, a judge may eventually dismiss the case that you're trying to build. (Sample opening sentences appear on the next page.)

The body of your report will appear in a section called the **narrative**. Here you'll describe what you saw and what you did, as well as the statements and actions of victims, witnesses, and suspects.

The narrative will end with a description of outcomes, called the **disposition**. Did you collect evidence, call an ambulance, make an arrest, make a referral to a community agency? All of these must be documented.

Actual reports vary, of course. Broadly speaking, they fall into four types, each with its own special features. Understanding these four types saves time and energy because you have a template to work from when you sit down to write. You won't have to worry about what to include or how to organize your information.

The First Sentence

Here's a standard opening sentence you can modify to use in your own reports:

At *time* on *date*, I, *rank, name, ID#, was dispatched to/was told about/saw* a *classification* at *location*.

These examples show how you can adapt the model sentence to your own reports:

At 0815 hours on 4 January 2009, I, Officer John Brown #546, was dispatched to a domestic disturbance at 301 Crown Place, Smithville.

At 1120 hours on 9 October 2010, I, Officer Susan Kimura #103, saw a blue Ford pick-up truck going north on Highway 29. The truck crossed the double line and drove in the southbound lane for about a mile.

At 1540 hours on 20 August 2010, a w/m inmate Tony Cliffs DC# 17542 told me, Officer Terry Winn #5437, about a fight at the weight pile near Baker Dorm.

At 2150 hours on 21 July 2010, I, Officer Mary Balodis #224, was dispatched to 1132 Short Street, Junction City, to investigate a burglary.

If you're filling out a paper form or using a laptop template, you probably won't need to put all this information into your opening sentence (unless your agency or institution asks you to do so).

Names

What about names? Officers sometimes wonder what to call a suspect who couldn't be identified right away. For example, suppose you clocked a car going 70 mph in a 45 mph zone. You didn't identify the driver until you'd stopped the car and asked for her driver's license. The general rule is that you can use the person's name right away. In some circumstances you can write, "later identified as Frances Palmore." Note how names are used in these examples:

At 0910 hours on 16 April 2010, I, Officer Barry Cameron, saw Billy Pemberton run out of the Sav-Mor store at 1520 Camellia Parkway carrying two six-packs of beer.

At 0440 hours on November 5 2008, I, Officer Sally Strathmore, saw a woman (later identified as Karen Huggins) lying on the sidewalk in front of First Baptist Church on Seaman Street.

The Narrative

For many officers, telling the story (in technical language, the *narrative*) is the most difficult part of writing a report. Often the story began before you got there. Instead of getting the story in one big chunk, like a TV show, you might get bits and pieces from several people. And they may start by telling you about events that happened in the middle of the story or even near the end.

How do you put all this together efficiently and effectively?

The answer is to use groupings. Remember, you're not writing a Hollywood script. It's perfectly OK (even recommended) to have a separate paragraph for each person's part of the story.

Suppose a juvenile, Jason, stole some valuable items from his parents and put them up for sale on eBay. You might get bits of the story from the mother, the father, a sister, and a grandmother. Use a separate paragraph for each one.

The examples below show how you could report what Jason's father and mother told you about their son's problems. (You'll notice that the information is written in bullet style, which you'll learn more about beginning on page 67.)

Mark Grant, Jason's father, told me:
- Jason had frequently been in trouble lately.
- Jason often withdrew into his room for hours at a time.
- Jason kept complaining that he didn't have enough money.

Karen Grant, Jason's mother, told me:

- She had noticed odd smells when she went into Jason's room to get his dirty laundry.
- A valuable ring was missing from her jewelry box at about seven o'clock this morning.
- She couldn't remember the last time she had seen the ring.

And so on. You'll see more examples in the next chapter.

Disposition

If you talk to experienced officers, you'll probably hear reminders about the importance of the final part of your report, where you tie up the loose ends. Did you tag, mark, photograph, package, or log any evidence? Were there injuries? If so, what did you see, and did an ambulance come? Did you suggest that a spouse spend the night with a friend, provide a victim's rights booklet, or make an arrest? Who transported and booked the suspect?

Incomplete details can create problems if a reporter asks for more information or an attorney challenges you in court later on. Ensure that *every report* you write is thorough and complete.

Exercise 4 Write a Report

Instructions: Write a report about the scenario below, following the numbered steps. When you're finished, compare your report to the sample on page 192 of the Answer Key.

1. Write an opening sentence.
2. Write a paragraph describing your arrival at the scene.
3. Write a paragraph describing what happened while you were there.
4. Write a concluding paragraph.

Scenario: At 1:30 p.m. today you were dispatched to 11 Clover Lane. When you arrived, you saw Karen Billings (WF, DOB 02/10/1999) standing in her front yard talking to a woman (WF, later identified as Joan Murray DOB 11/23/1932) in a blue bathrobe and bedroom slippers.

Karen told you that she had gone outside to mail a letter. She saw Joan Murray walking along the sidewalk, looking anxiously from side to side. She looked lost. Karen asked for her name and address, but Joan didn't respond. She kept talking about wanting to find her canary, Buttermilk. Karen moved into the neighborhood recently and did not recognize Joan. She called the police.

While you and Karen were talking, a man came running down the sidewalk, waving his hands. He grabbed Joan's hand and explained that he was her husband (Stephen Murray, DOB 5/15/1930). Joan has Alzheimer's. She apparently opened the front door and walked out of the house.

You gave Stephen the telephone number for Elder Services and instructed him to install a hook and eye on all doors to prevent Joan from leaving the house again. Stephen escorted Joan to their home at 35 Clover Lane.

Exercise 5 Why Is the Report Necessary?

Instructions: No charges were filed in the previous incident. Why is it important to write a report about what happened? Give as many reasons as you can. When you're finished, check your answers on page 191.

Chapter 6

Types of Reports

The field of criminal justice is infinitely varied: You never know what you're going to encounter. Many officers say that this variety is one of the best features of a criminal justice career.

It's also true, however, that the variety of situations can create confusion when you're writing a report. How do you organize your information? How can you ensure that you haven't omitted anything important?

Despite their variety, reports generally can be classified into **four types**. When you familiarize yourself with these types of reports, you'll always have a mental outline to follow when you sit down to write.

Another benefit of knowing these classifications is that the types build on one another. Once you know how to do a Type 1 report (the simplest), you'll need to make only a few additions when you do a Type 2 report. The same is true for Types 3 and 4.

A Closer Look at the Four Types

In Type 1, the officer is primarily a recorder. She arrives after the crime or incident has occurred and takes down the facts.

In Type 2, the officer is a participant. In addition to recording what happened, he performs an investigation—questioning neighbors, looking for an entry point, taking fingerprints, or looking for other evidence. (The police report on page 16 is a Type 2 report.)

In Type 3, the officer becomes involved in an active crime scene. She settles a fight, separates two angry spouses, apprehends a thief, or plays some other role.

In Type 4, the officer is the first person on the scene. He suspects that a crime is being committed, starts the investigation, and takes an active part in resolving it. (The corrections report on page 17 is a Type 4 report.) Probable cause is an important issue in Type 4 reports: You must establish that you had a right to intervene in the situation.

On the next page, a chart compares and contrasts the four types of reports. You can read sample reports of all four types beginning on page 42.

TYPES OF REPORTS

Type of report	Officer's Role	Information required	Challenges
Type 1 **No action is taken** (includes incident reports)	Look, listen, and write	Record what happened before you arrived	Accuracy, professionalism, and completeness
Type 2 **A reported crime requires investigation**	Look, listen, write, and investigate	Record what happened, plus the results of your investigation	Demonstrate that procedures were followed, and include results of your investigation, even if they were negative
Type 3 **A reported crime requires investigation and intervention**	Look, listen, write, investigate, and take an active role in resolving the situation	Record what happened, plus the results of your investigation, plus the nature of your intervention (arrest?)	Three stories must be blended in your report: **History** (what happened before you arrived) **Developing story** (what the you saw and heard) **Your story** (how the you handled the incident)
Type 4 **You (not a citizen) set the case in motion yourself**	Initiate the investigation and follow through	Tell why you got involved, what happened, the results of your investigation, and the outcome	Probable cause may be an issue. Justify your involvement, and document that you followed procedures correctly

Looking at a Type 1 Report

Notice that the action (someone stole a bicycle) happened *before the officer arrived.*

At 5:22 p.m. on May 12, 2010, I was dispatched to 239 Carol Avenue regarding a theft. Lawrence Cooper (DOB 7-15-1987) reported that his son David's bicycle had been stolen.

Cooper told me:

- David (DOB 11-04-2001) had brought the bicycle into the carport the evening before (May 11).
- The bicycle wasn't locked.
- The bicycle is a blue Sears bicycle with black tires and black handlebars.
- The bicycle is three years old.

David went to the carport after school to ride the bicycle. He saw the bicycle was missing. When his father came home, David told him that the bike had been stolen. Lawrence called the police at 5:20.

No one was home all day. Neither David nor Lawrence knows when the bicycle was stolen. They don't remember whether it was in the carport this morning. They did not hear any unusual noises last night.

Looking at a Type 2 Report

In addition to recording what happened earlier, the officer undertakes an investigation by looking for fingerprints and the point of entry and questioning a neighbor.

On April 9, 2010, at 9:45 a.m., I, Officer Tom Morgan, was dispatched to 2170 Powell Street to investigate a burglary. I met with Frank Gaines, the homeowner who had reported the burglary.

Gaines told me he lives alone. He was out of town on business when the burglary happened. He had left on April 5, at approximately 6:15 p.m. and returned on April 9 at approximately 8:45 a.m. Because he used his car for the trip, there was no car in his carport when he was gone.

He said because he left during daylight, he hadn't thought to leave any lights burning. He is a sales representative for Pfizer, and many people know that he often does business from home and makes sales trips.

When he returned from his trip, he saw a broken window over the kitchen table.

The following items are missing from his home office:

- Dell Alienware computer   Serial #1534920814
- HP Laserjet Printer Serial #23179085
- Brother IntelliFax-41003 machine Serial #5656778912

I lifted latent fingerprints from the desk in Gaines' home office. In the kitchen I saw fragments of glass on the floor. The broken window is about 4½ feet high by 6 feet across. I walked through the rest of the house and saw no other evidence of the break-in. All doors and all other windows are intact.

I went to the back yard and saw that the broken kitchen window is about three feet from the ground. I photographed the broken window from inside the kitchen and from the back yard.

Gaines told me that he is friendly with a retired neighbor who lives next door, and she keeps an eye on his house when he is away on business.

I questioned the neighbor (Anna Morgan, 2164 Powell Street). She told me:

- Her dog started barking at about 2 a.m. on April 7.
- She had a headache and did not feel like looking outside.
- She put the dog into her guest bedroom so she could get some sleep.

Nothing else unusual happened while Gaines was away.

I suggested that Gaines invest in an alarm system, since he is often away from home, and I emphasized the importance of leaving lights on when he is away.

I took the fingerprints to the Evidence Room at approximately 10:35 a.m. on April 9.

Looking at a Type 3 Report

In addition to recording the facts and investigating, the officer becomes part of the story: She separates the angry spouses, stops an assault, and arrests the assailant.

At approximately 7:45 p.m. on 4 January 2010, I, Officer Janice Ruiz #5407, was dispatched to a domestic disturbance at 301 Crown Place, Worthington.

I arrived at the house at 7:53 p.m. A woman was standing on the front lawn. She (Karen Lynch, WF, DOB 3/14/74) said that she was a neighbor (295 Crown Place). She said she called the police when she heard screams coming from the house. I told her I would handle the problem.

I knocked on the front door and called out "Police officer." I heard a woman's voice yell, "I hate you! I hate you!" I heard a man's voice yell, "Shut your trap, you stupid bitch." No one answered the door. I tried the knob. The door was unlocked, and I entered the living room.

A woman (Jane Brown, WF, DOB 8/15/81) was sitting on the sofa. There was a red bruise on her right cheek. Her lips were trembling. Her face was wet, and her eye makeup was smeared. A man (Tim Brown, WM, DOB 11/13/79) was standing over her. His fists were clenched.

I said, "What's the problem here?" and asked Tim to sit down in an armchair. Tim told me, "Leave us alone. This is our house. It's none of your business." I again asked him to sit down, and he went to the armchair.

Jane Brown told me:

- She and Tim are married.
- She came home late from work and rushed to cook dinner.
- Tim became angry when he came to the table.
- He said he hated her cooking.
- Tim threw his pork chop at the wall.
- She jumped up from her seat and yelled that nothing she did was ever good enough for him.
- He slapped her on her right cheek.

Tim Brown told me:

- Jane cared more about her job and spending money than making a nice home.
- They had been fighting frequently.
- He slapped her and would do it again.

Tim Brown then walked over to the sofa and slapped Jane on her right cheek. He said, "I'm in charge here."

I told Tim to go into the kitchen and sit down at the table there. He went into the kitchen and sat down. I called for a backup.

Officer Susan Clark #423 arrived at 8:19 p.m. She photographed Jane's face with her department cell phone camera and handed Jane a victim's booklet. Jane said she did not need medical attention. Clark explained state attorney procedures to Jane.

I arrested Tim and read him the Miranda warning from my card. Clark and I put him into my patrol car, and I drove him to the station.

Looking at a Type 4 Report

Here *the officer is the initiator* and must provide *probable cause* when writing the report. When Officer Warner writes his report, he will explain in detail why he became involved in the incident between Coffley and Sims.

At 0815 hours on 4 January, 2010, on the sidewalk in front of C Dorm, I, Officer Clint Warner #14256, saw inmate Charles Pandit R-23165 extend his right leg in front of another inmate, Robert Sims R-11725, who was headed into the dorm. Sims stumbled and dropped the soft drink he was carrying. Some of the liquid splashed on Pandit's uniform.

Pandit turned to Sims, grabbed his left arm, and shouted, "You did that on purpose!"

I was standing about 5 yards behind Pandit and Sims. I told Pandit that I had seen the incident and was going to write a disciplinary report. I radioed for assistance. When Officer Aoki arrived at C Dorm, we escorted Pandit to disciplinary confinement.

Exercise 6 Four Types of Reports

Instructions: Think of the type of report you would write for the situations below. Number each Type 1, Type 2, Type 3, or Type 4. (Referring to the chart on page 41 may be helpful.) Answers appear on page 193.

_____ 1. You stop a fight in the parking lot of a baseball stadium.

_____2. A citizen reports a stolen boat.

_____3. The manager of a convenience store says she's caught a 14-year-old boy who stole a six-pack of beer.

_____4.   A woman reports that her wallet was taken from her car while she was visiting a friend in the hospital.

_____5. A citizen comes home from work and realizes that someone broke into his house and stole his computer.

_____6. You stop a driver who went through a stop sign without stopping, and the driver fails a sobriety test.

_____7. A patient assaults a technician in an emergency room.

_____8. In a correctional institution, you spot something shiny under a shrub near the chow hall; it's a pocketknife half buried in the soil.

_____9. During a routine locker check in a correctional institution, you find a small bottle of wine—the size served on airplanes.

_____10. A driver reports that she just drove past a collision.

Exercise 7 More Practice with Types of Reports

Instructions: Think of the type of report you would write for the situations below. Number each Type 1, Type 2, Type 3, or Type 4. (Referring to the chart on page 41 may be helpful.) Answers appear on page 194.

____1. You're dispatched to a park to break up a fight at a family reunion.

____2. You're an officer in a correctional institution, where a nurse discovers that painkillers have been stolen from the locked medicine cabinet.

____3. A man reports that his daughter has run away with her boyfriend.

____4. You find a pornographic magazine under the mattress in an inmate's cell.

____5. You and your partner are dispatched to a domestic disturbance called in by a neighbor. When you arrive, husband and wife blame each other for the incident.

Chapter 7

Objectivity

Opinions have no place in a criminal justice report.

If you're new to report writing, this objectivity requirement may take some getting used to. It's natural to want to state that the man in the red plaid jacket was behaving suspiciously or seemed inebriated.

It's tempting to write that the kitchen window was probably the point of entry in the break-in. You may want to say that the inmate was disrespectful when you confronted him about disrupting the count. In everyday life we often think along these lines.

But inserting these opinions, hunches, guesses, and predictions into a criminal justice report risks labeling you as unprofessional. Even worse, that kind of writing can get you into trouble in court.

A skillful attorney can use vague descriptions ("The suspect was nervous") to cast doubt on your judgment, trip you up on the witness stand, or convince the judge that you did not have probable cause for getting involved in the first place.

Objective (factual) reports make you look professional, and they're especially useful in court. After a long time has passed, you may not remember details about what you saw. If they're plainly stated in your report, you'll have no problem testifying. And many officers say that good reports can help keep a case from landing in court. An attorney who sees that you've convincingly stated the facts may decide not to challenge what you did.

Start thinking about ways you can *describe* (rather than label) a person who is nervous, inebriated, sarcastic, belligerent, aggressive, disrespectful, frightened, or disoriented. For example, instead of writing "Jones was disrespectful," you could write what Jones actually said, *showing* that he was disrespectful: "Jones told me, "If you knew what you were doing, the count would be finished by now.""

Here are some examples:

Opinion	Observable Fact
sloppy	wearing a torn and faded shirt
defiant	looked away and said nothing when I questioned him
afraid	lips were trembling and hands were shaking
obviously drunk	failed two sobriety tests
reckless	was doing 45 mph in a 20 mph zone and went through a stop sign
crazy	zigzagged across the sidewalk while talking to herself

Writing an Objective Report

In the past, officers used to be counseled to avoid using names in their reports. Everyone was identified as Victim 1, Victim 2, Suspect 1, Suspect 2, and so on. The reasoning was that numbers do not have emotions and prejudices, so the report's objectivity was guaranteed.

Many agencies have dropped this practice, for a number of good reasons. First, it slows down the writing process. Busy officers have to keep stopping mid-sentence to look back and see if, say, Manny Sanchez was Witness 1 or Witness 2.

Second, it increases the likelihood of mistakes, especially in a complex report. A tired officer writes a 3 instead of a 4—and months later, in court, disaster strikes when the error becomes apparent.

Third, it can create problems when you're preparing to testify in court. Busy officers don't want to waste precious time trying to untangle a puzzling report. It's much easier to refresh your memory if you have actual names in front of you.

Most important, verbal tricks don't make an officer objective and professional. A biased or dishonest officer can write "Victim 1, Victim 2" just as easily as a competent one. The same principle applies to passive voice (more about this on page 71) and the old-fashioned rule that you should write "this officer" instead of "I."

Professionalism comes from a commitment to integrity and a thorough education in the best criminal justice procedures. It requires character and commitment. Don't let anyone fool you into thinking that rewriting a sentence can magically turn a bad officer into a good one. It just isn't so.

Objectivity is a professional quality that requires constant practice and self-monitoring. In everyday life we constantly draw conclusions, express opinions, and make inferences. Those activities do not belong in a criminal justice report, however.

Here's one example: Suppose you were investigating a break-in. A man tells you that he suspects his ex-wife, who's very angry about their recent split. You walk through his apartment and see plenty of evidence to back up his suspicions: Overturned bureau drawers, a broken mirror, two sofa cushions slashed with a knife. Yes, he's the victim of a woman who feels wronged.

Or is he? Could he have staged the break-in himself to try to have her put into jail? Or could another someone else have done the damage? Is it possible that a neighbor suspected there were valuables in the apartment and came looking for them?

The officer's job is to record only the facts—in this case, what the victim said and the damage in the apartment. Opinions ("I definitely think it was his ex-wife" or "I got the feeling he was lying") have no place in a criminal justice report.

Similarly, don't assume you know what a suspect is thinking. A statement like this one would not be acceptable in court: "Wilson obviously was planning to escape through the bathroom window." Stick to describing exactly what the suspect did: "Wilson ran into the bathroom and locked the door. I heard the click of the lock, and the knob did not move when I tried to turn it. The bathroom had a window about four feet from the floor."

Closely related to objectivity is the issue of *sensitivity*—another hallmark of a professional officer. Insensitive language should be omitted from your report *unless you're quoting someone's exact words*. Here are some guidelines:

- Use *boy* and *girl* only to refer to children.
- Do not use street slang for minorities or disabled persons.
- Do not use sexually charged language to refer to women (*broad, stacked, bombshell*, etc.)
- Use neutral language when you're referring to people as a group. Appropriate terminology includes "low-income" (rather than "poor" or "lower-class"), "persons with a history of mental illness," "persons with epilepsy," and "gays and lesbians." Street language such as "crazy," "spastic," and similar terminology is not appropriate for an officer.

Exercise 8 Objectivity

Instructions: Put a check √ in front of the sentences that are objective. Put an X in front of any sentences that lack objectivity. Answers appear on page 194.

_____1. On the east side of 10th Street I saw a WM in jeans and a red flannel shirt who was behaving suspiciously.

_____2. Albert Johnson threatened his wife.

_____3. I smelled an alcoholic beverage on Carol Johnson's breath.

_____4. Inmate Palmer approached me with his fists clenched.

_____5. I saw what might be a weapon in his left pocket.

_____6. I saw an irregular bulge in his left pocket.

_____7. Overturned bureau drawers were lying on the bedroom floor.

_____8. When I looked into the back porch, I saw evidence of a break-in.

_____9. Inmate Chapman seemed nervous when I walked into his cell.

_____10. Harmon's hands trembled when I asked him to open his locker.

Chapter 8

What To Omit

Officers often worry (and rightly so) about leaving something important out of a report. But it's also true that some things *don't* belong in a report. Here are some examples:

- Opinions (Because of Mrs. Gupta's age, I knew she might not have heard the noise outside.)
- Conclusions (I decided the suspect had probably exited through the bedroom window.)
- Generalizations (Brakus seemed confused.)
- Hunches (The witness was probably lying.)
- Insensitivity (Mr. Nagy is obviously crazy and needs to be in an institution.)

You also need to watch for writing practices that don't belong in a modern criminal justice report. The three practices discussed below can lead to inefficiency and errors.

1. Passive voice

Stick to active voice unless you're describing an action by an unknown person. Passive voice can be wordy and confusing (with the exception noted below).

Here's an example of what can happen if you consistently use passive voice. Suppose you wrote, "Clark was questioned about his activities Monday morning." Now fast-forward to a court hearing three months later. You may not remember whether it was you or your partner who did the questioning—and your report won't help you.

It's OK to use passive voice when you really don't know who performed an action: "A wallet and a diamond ring were taken from the nightstand." Otherwise you should stick to active voice. (You can learn more about passive voice beginning on page 71.)

2. Jargon

Expressions like "I Mirandized him," "I Baker-acted her," and "I processed the area" can confuse outsiders who read your reports—and it gives the impression that you were in too much of a hurry to explain clearly what you did. (See page 167.) These sentences are more professional:

- I read him his rights from my Miranda card.
- I took her into custody and began Baker Act proceedings.
- I examined the front and back doors. I found pry marks by the outside door handle on the back door.

3. Unnecessary repetition

Needless words waste time and leaves you open to factual and grammatical errors. You don't need to write down everything you said when you're questioning a witness or a suspect. Omit expressions like "Then I asked him," "I followed up with," "My next question was."

Compare the two versions below:

I asked her what time she got home from work. She said 5:20 p.m. I asked what happened. She said she noticed the open window and got worried. I asked if she was sure it had been closed when she left that morning. She said yes, she was sure it had been closed. REPETITIOUS

I asked her what happened. She said she got home from work at 5:20 p.m. She saw the open window and got worried. She was sure it had been closed when she left that morning. BETTER

Sometimes, of course, you'll need to record a person's exact words. It's usually a good idea to record everything that a suspect says, word-for-word, and anything that a witness heard a suspect say. Use quotation marks in both your notes and your report to signify that you recorded the statements accurately.

Develop the habit of checking your reports over to see how you can improve them. Over time, you'll see a dramatic and very satisfying improvement.

Exercise 9 Rewrite These Sentences

Instructions: These are excerpts from police and corrections reports. Use the guidelines in this chapter to rewrite these excerpts to meet modern report writing standards. You may need to invent some details. Suggested answers appear in the Answer Key on page 195.

1. Inmate Joseph Curry was ordered by this officer to empty his pockets.

2. Pate appeared to be nervous. I suspected he was lying. I asked him where the sealed cartons in the back seat came from, hoping he would start to contradict himself.

3. The teenagers were rude when I told them their skateboards were damaging the park benches.

4. I asked Johnson what had happened. She told me that a man and woman walked into her store and started arguing. I asked what they were arguing about.
She said the woman wanted to buy a six-pack of beer, but the man said she needed to cut back on her drinking.
I asked Johnson what happened next. She said the woman grabbed a six-pack of Budweiser. I asked what the man had done in response. Johnson said he pushed her against the door of the cooler and took the six-pack away from her.

5. Inmate Rogers exploded when I found a jar of Nescafe coffee under her pillow and took possession of it.

6. Cooper was informed that he was under arrest. He was Mirandized and placed in the back of this officer's patrol car.

Chapter 9

Quoting Exact Words

Police and correctional officers frequently write down what victims, witnesses, and suspects say. Getting the words right is vital. Sometimes it can even mean the difference between an acquittal and a successful prosecution.

(Getting the punctuation right is just as important because it showcases your professionalism. Instruction on using quotation marks begins on page 125.)

Developing your ability to concentrate is the first step towards learning how to record people's statements accurately. Most people spend most of their time thinking about their own lives and their own problems. In a conversation, they're usually thinking about what they're going to say next. As an officer, you need to redirect your thinking to the situation at hand, observing and retaining everything that's said.

It's equally important to strengthen your ability to remember. Here's one way to do it: When you watch TV or listen to the radio, try to repeat exactly what you heard. Keep practicing, and strive to increase the number of words you can retain in your memory. After a conversation or a meeting, see if you can repeat what each person said.

Here are three suggestions for accurately recording what you hear when you talk to witnesses, victims, and suspects:

1. Be specific.

"Inmate Jones threatened me" isn't good enough. You need to record *exactly* what he said and did:

Inmate Jones took two steps forward, made a fist, and said, "You'd better watch your back, because I'm not gonna quit until I get you for this."
CORRECT

2. Don't shy away from writing down slang, blasphemy, indecent words, and racial slurs when you're quoting a witness or suspect.

Record *exactly* what the person said, word-for-word. Some suspects use the same phrases and expressions over and over. Your report might provide the missing piece needed to identify and arrest a suspect.

3. Don't comment or editorialize about what was said.

Observations like "I was shocked" or "I knew she was lying" don't belong in a professional report.

Exercise 10 What Did They Say?

Instructions: Put a check √ in front of each sentence that effectively records what a witness or suspect said. Mark ineffective sentences with an X. Answers appear on page 196.

_____1. Patricia said that her husband was abusive to her.

_____2. Mark said that his wife repeatedly criticized his earning power in front of their guests. When he asked her to stop, she threw a bowl of mashed potatoes at him.

_____3. Reilly told me that he had been at work when the burglary was committed.

_____4. Jones responded to my accusation with an alibi.

_____5. Linda was obviously covering up for her husband when she said he'd been home all evening.

_____6. Hayley said she had been to Walgreen's, Radio Shack, and the First National Bank that morning.

____7. Dennis showed signs of dementia when he tried to recount what had happened.

____8. Dennis spoke slowly, in broken sentences. Several times he repeated himself. Twice there were long pauses while he searched for the word he wanted. Finally he said he'd been watching TV when the doorbell rang.

Chapter 10

How Helpful is OJT?

OJT (on-the-job training) is how professionals in many fields learn their jobs. Talk to successful people in almost any career, and they're likely to say that their higher education was all well and good, but they really learned how to do their jobs by imitating other people at work.

Sometimes that's a good thing, sometimes not. It can mean that professionals are still stuck in the-way-we've-always-done-it instead of updating procedures and policies in light of new research and technology.

Criminal justice is a case in point. Laptops can make report writing much more efficient because officers can enter some of the information into boxes instead of writing out whole sentences. But a supervisor who was trained to write reports in pen and ink may not see the benefits of adapting.

The opening sentence in a narrative is one example. In bygone days, when police reports were written on blank pieces of paper, it made sense to cram as much information as possible into the first sentence: "At 0842 hours on 8/07/10 I, Officer Carole Lynch, #547, was dispatched to a burglary at 1512 Carmen Boulevard."

But what if your laptop provides spaces for the time, date, type of call, address, and your official ID? There's no need to re-enter them. But the tradition lives on in many agencies.

Four features of good report writing are especially prone to be forgotten by officers who received their training through OJT:

1. Active Voice

There are still people who believe that officers instantly become more ethical and objective when they write in passive voice (*The door was checked for pry marks*) instead of active voice (*I checked the door for pry marks*). The truth, unfortunately, is that there are no shortcuts in criminal justice and no easy ways to turn mediocre officers into top-notch professionals. (For more about active voice versus passive voice, go to page 71.)

2. Personal Pronouns

The same mistaken belief lingers on about words like "I" and "me": You'll be more objective and professional if you avoid "I" and "me" and write "this officer" instead. This too is wishful thinking. Think about people you've known who are biased, opinionated, or prejudiced. Could you transform those people just by changing a couple of words in a sentence? The obvious answer is *no*.

3. Bullet Style

Many agencies are discovering that they like bullet style (explained in detail on page 67) because it's easier than writing complete sentences. Other benefits are that bullet style is more compact, easier to organize, and quicker to read—a particular advantage when you're getting ready to testify in court.

But some agencies continue to resist making the change to bullet style. What to do? Stick to the policies your supervisor or agency prefers—but, at the same time, make a resolution to be on the lookout for better ways to write reports. When the time comes for you to be promoted, you'll be ready to show genuine leadership in the area of report writing.

4. Timesaving Word Choices

Report writing is a time-intensive task. Why make the job even more burdensome with unnecessary and time-wasting words? There's no need to write "the abovementioned witness" when you can simply use the name: *Paula Olsen*. And words like *respective* and *individual* can often be omitted:

> The neighbors returned to their respective houses. WORDY
> The neighbors returned to their houses. BETTER

> Individual members will receive a dues notice next week.
> WORDY
> Members will receive a dues notice next week. BETTER

To learn more about effective word choices, go to page 167.

Exercise 11 Think about OJT

Instructions: Write a list of helpful things you've learned about criminal justice a) from your own experience and b) from other officers. When you're finished, put a check √ in front of each item that you think might be useful to future officers.

Chapter 11

Bullet Style

Bullet style has become popular in business writing, for good reasons: It's an efficient and readable way to organize groups of facts.

Bullet style is equally useful in criminal justice reports. Since officers tend to use the same headings again and again, bullet style can save time and help eliminate errors. The headings used in bullet style will help you organize your thoughts and remember details you might otherwise overlook.

What does bullet style look like? Actually you've seen it a number of times already in this book, in the reports on pages 42 - 46. Here's an example:

Anne told me:

- She and Davis were living together.
- Davis didn't like Anne's son, Cole.
- Davis and Cole fought about Cole's grades in school.
- Davis hit Cole on the left side of his face.
- Anne grabbed Davis' arm and screamed, "Stop it! Stop it!"
- Davis hit her on her mouth.

Comparing a Traditional Paragraph to Bullet Style

Let's take a look at a paragraph in conventional sentence style that you might see in a corrections report:

I searched Dickert's locker. I found three $20 bills between the pages of a *Sports Illustrated* magazine. There was a pair of dice in the pocket of a uniform shirt. I found five $10 bills between the pages of his Bible. I found three unopened decks of cards at the bottom of a laundry bag.

Now let's look at the same information presented in bullet style:

I searched Dickert's locker and found:

- three $20 bills between the pages of a *Sports Illustrated* magazine
- a pair of dice in the pocket of a uniform shirt
- five $10 bills between the pages of his Bible
- three unopened decks of cards at the bottom of a laundry bag

---

Useful Headings for Bullet Style

When I entered the room, I saw:

[Name] told me:

I dusted these items for fingerprints:

I performed the following sobriety tests:

The following people had keys to the store:

I tagged these items as evidence and took them to the Evidence Room:

Bullet style isn't difficult to learn. You can start by practicing writing down everyday information in bullets. You'll find bullet style extremely useful when you write your reports.

Exercise 12 Using Bullet Style

Instructions: Rewrite the paragraphs below in bullet style. Suggested answers appear on page 197.

1. Patterson noticed many things were wrong when she entered her bedroom. Dresser drawers were overturned and emptied on the floor. The lock on her jewelry box was broken. The jewelry box was emptied on her bed. Her favorite gold necklace was missing. A platinum diamond ring was missing.

2. After talking to the bartender (WM Tom Tippin, DOB 12/06/1986), I entered a private room in the back and saw a WM (Clarence Coppin, DOB 4/12/1984) a BF server (Doris James, DOB 5/03/1987), a young girl (Ginny Coppin, DOB 9/12/2002), and a WF (Susan Coppin, DOB 1/19/1986). I heard Susan scream, "Get the hell out of here." Although Ginny was kicking Clarence's legs, he paid no attention to her. While all this was going on, Doris James was picking up broken pieces of glass from the floor.

3. Dominguez said he'd left his wallet on the front seat while he ran into McDonald's to use the bathroom. His friend Galleti was sitting in the passenger seat. When Dominguez returned to his car, both Galleti and the wallet were gone.

Chapter 12

Active Voice or Passive Voice?

Earlier in this book, on page 55, you saw that agencies today prefer active voice to passive voice. It might be helpful to take a closer look at both types of sentences to see why agencies are moving away from passive voice.

First, passive voice is old-fashioned; today's professional officers tend not use it any more. Second, passive voice can be confusing and inefficient because it doesn't state *who* did *what*. For a better understanding of these problems, let's look at two examples, one in active voice, and the other in passive voice:

> Dickert's locker was searched, and three $20 bills were found inside a copy of *Sports Illustrated* magazine. PASSIVE

> I searched Dickert's locker and found three $20 bills inside a copy of *Sports Illustrated* magazine. ACTIVE

An obvious problem with "Dickert's locker was searched" is that the reader doesn't know *who* searched it—opening the institution up to problems later on if there's a question about the search or the charges.

In the past, criminal justice professionals sometimes argued that passive voice ensured objectivity. If only it were that easy! Unfortunately, that simply is not true.

In the example you just read, imagine for a moment that the correctional officer who searched Dickert's locker was dishonest, either planting the cash in the inmate's magazine or lying about what was found. Will writing in passive voice cause the officer to generate an honest report in this situation? The obvious answer is *no*.

Be careful, however, not to be fooled into "correcting" sentences that were right in the first place. Make sure a sentence is really passive before you change it. Compare these two examples:

The suspects were questioned. PASSIVE VOICE

While we were questioning the suspects, Officer Brown arrived at the scene.
 ACTIVE VOICE

"We were questioning" is **active** voice because you know that **we** were doing it. The second sentence does not need to be corrected. (The first one is passive and should be rewritten.)

Finally, note that there's one situation in which passive voice is useful and appropriate: When you don't know who was responsible for a particular act. Take a look at these two examples:

The liquor store was broken into late last night. Two cases of wine were taken. PASSIVE VOICE acceptable

Since you don't know who broke in and took the wine, passive voice is acceptable.

Passive voice can also be useful if you don't want to embarrass a person for something he or she has done:

Unwashed dishes have been left in the break room three times this week. PASSIVE VOICE acceptable

Exercise 13 Using Active and Passive Voice

Instructions: Put a check √ in front of each active-voice sentence. Mark each passive-voice sentence with an X, and rewrite it in active voice. (You may have to invent names as you rewrite the sentences.) Check your answers against the Answer Key on page 198.

_____1. Jones was seen running away from the convenience store.

_____2. Jones was carrying a six-pack of beer and a bottle of white wine.

_____3. Three sobriety tests were administered.

_____4. Patterson was looking in his wallet for his driver's license.

_____5. Both witnesses were questioned.

_____6. Finch was having difficulty answering the questions.

_____7. Chief Clancy and Major Hansen rewrote the procedure.

_____8. The procedure was rewritten two years ago.

_____9. I was hoping to take a week of vacation in late August.

_____10. The wallet was found under the driver's seat.

_____11. The mayor will be attending Lieutenant Cohen's retirement ceremony.

_____12. Luis is interested in forensics.

_____13. Scientists in crime labs are being paid top salaries right now.

___14. Three years ago, Luis was working in a low-paying service job.

___15. He was told there wasn't much of a future for him there.

Chapter 13

Online Resources for Officers

The Internet provides many free websites about writing that are useful to criminal justice officers. The websites listed here will prove useful throughout your career, so it's a good idea to bookmark and use them often. All are free.

1. *The Uniform Crime Reporting Handbook* from the FBI

You're probably familiar with this handbook already. You can download it as a .pdf at www.fbi.gov/ucr/ucr.htm (scroll down to find the Handbook link). Here's how the FBI describes the UCR:

> The UCR *Handbook* outlines the classification and scoring guidelines that law enforcement agencies use to report crimes to the UCR Program. In addition, it contains offense and arrest reporting forms and an explanation of how to complete them. The Handbook also provides definitions of all UCR offenses.

Even if you're not compiling statistics, the UCR is invaluable: It clarifies criminal justice terminology, provides scenarios to discuss, and explains how professionals classify various crimes.

2. www.Dictionary.com

Besides offering definitions, this website compares what various dictionaries say about a particular word or phrase, and it sometimes offers usage notes.

3. www.PlainLanguage.gov

Jargon and gobbledygook waste time, create confusion, and make a bad impression on your readers. This government-sponsored website provides many easy-to-use resources to help you write more clearly and efficiently.

4. www.YourPoliceWrite.com

Created for criminal justice officers, this website provides a thorough review of grammar, usage, and special issues related to report writing.

5. www.WritewithJean.com

This website provides ongoing instruction about a wide variety of writing issues.

6. Workspace.Office.Live.com

(Note that there's no "www.") This is a career-building website that allows you to collaborate with colleagues. If you're working on a job-related writing project, you can post your draft here and allow colleagues to log in to make additions and edits. There's no need to email drafts to one another: Everything is securely (and privately) stored online. This is a great professional tool that you'll use often as you move up the career ladder.

7. www.FlipDrive.com

Here's another career-building website. You can securely store documents and photographs here. If you move to another computer, just log on to access a project you're working on. You don't need to carry a flash drive around—and you don't have to worry about losing it.

8. www.Evernote.com

Say good-bye to Post-It notes—although they're handy, they're also easily lost. This free, privacy-protected website sorts and stores any information you want to save. You can access the information from any computer with Internet access. Evernote allows you to clean out your desk and set up a quick, reliable system to find important information.

9. www.Passpack.com

This isn't really a writers' website, but it's a lifesaver for many professionals. You can securely store passwords here, free of charge, and access them from any computer with Internet access. This is a great website if you have accounts with many websites, and it's especially useful if you travel often: You don't have to worry about carrying (and possibly losing) a list of passwords.

Exercise 14 Exploring Online Resources

Instructions: Choose two of these websites and explore what they have to offer you. Then write a brief explanation of how you would use each website you selected.

Section III

Solving Sentence Problems

Chapter 14

Fragments

The first requirement for a sentence also happens to be the most important requirement: Completeness. English grammar is full of obscure rules that you might be able to break without getting caught. But writing an incomplete sentence (also called a fragment) is a serious error that most good readers will notice immediately—to your detriment.

Fortunately there's an easy way to ensure that your sentences will probably meet this **completeness** requirement: Start every sentence with a person, place, or thing. To put it differently: If you're unsure of your writing skills, take the safe route. Avoid writing complicated sentences that can get you into trouble.

Take a look at the two paragraphs below. They state the same information, but the first version contains several fragments. The second version is less fancy—but every sentence is correct.

Version 1 (fragments are underlined):

We separated Jennings and Cooper. I took Jennings into the kitchen. Asked her what had happened. Trying to decide who had started the fight. Jennings told me that Cooper came home from work in a bad mood. She tried to cheer him up. Although, she suspected that trouble was coming. Because he didn't seem like himself lately. Seemed like something was eating at him.

Version 2 (all sentences are correct):

We separated Jennings and Cooper. I took Jennings into the kitchen. I asked her what had happened. I was trying to decide who had started the fight. Jennings told me that Cooper came home from work in a bad mood. She tried to cheer him up although she suspected that trouble was coming because he didn't seem like himself lately. It seemed like something was eating at him

A Closer Look at Fragments

The following tips will help you avoid writing fragments (incomplete sentences):

- Remember that most fragments appear at the start of a paragraph or the beginning of a section of a report. Double-check those spots for completeness.
- Be careful with sentences beginning with words like *first*, *next*, and *finally*: Fragments often creep in there.
- Check every sentence that begins with an *–ing* word: Such sentences are notorious for turning into fragments.
- Starting each sentence with a person, place, or thing is good insurance against fragments.
- Avoiding "red flag" words at the beginning of a sentence is also good insurance. In general, avoid starting sentences with *like*, *who*, *which*, and *such as*.

What Do Fragments Look Like?

Here is a report containing several fragments (underlined):

Palm Court is an assisted-living facility administered by the Methodist Church. Administrators at Palm Court met with representatives from several community agencies to discuss enhancing security at the facility. They noted several concerns.

<u>First, unauthorized visitors.</u> Palm Court encourages visits from family and friends. Because the staff wants to maintain a welcoming atmosphere, there is no sign-in procedure for visitors. Several thefts have occurred because outsiders come and go freely. <u>Entering and leaving the building without being stopped and questioned.</u>

Second, inadequate locks. In the past, Palm Court did not install sturdy locks on apartment doors. Worrying that residents would accidentally lock themselves out. As a result, residents are not adequately protected against intruders.

Third, untrained staff. Palm Court has done a good job recruiting caring workers who are sensitive to the needs of elderly residents. But staff members have not been taught how to maintain a secure facility. Having proven procedures to protect residents and their possessions from harm.

And here is the same report with the fragments corrected (in *italics*):

Palm Court is an assisted-living facility administered by the Methodist Church. Administrators at Palm Court met with representatives from several community agencies to discuss enhancing security at the facility. They noted several concerns.

The first problem is unauthorized visitors. Palm Court encourages visits from family and friends. Because the staff wants to maintain a welcoming atmosphere, there is no sign-in procedure for visitors. Several thefts have occurred because outsiders come and go freely, entering and leaving the building without being stopped and questioned.

The second problem is inadequate locks. In the past, Palm Court did not install sturdy locks on apartment doors. Administrators were afraid that residents would accidentally lock themselves out. As a result, residents are not adequately protected against intruders.

The third problem is untrained staff. Palm Court has done a good job recruiting caring workers who are sensitive to the needs of elderly residents. But staff members have not been taught how to maintain a secure facility. *It's important to establish proven procedures to protect residents and their possessions from harm.*

Exercise 15 Fragments

Instructions: Put an X in front of each fragment, and then rewrite it so that it is complete. When you're finished, check your answers on page 199.

_____1. Inmate Armstrong asked to go to sickbay at 9:30 this morning.

_____2. Complained of a bad headache and nausea.

_____3. Although, five minutes earlier he'd been joking and smiling.

_____4. Noticing that he kept glancing at Inmate Opeya.

_____5. Who was working next to him.

_____6. Officer Link told me Opeya and Armstrong got into a shoving match.

_____7. Armstrong wanted to avoid a fight by going to sickbay.

_____8. Like other inmates who try to manipulate supervisors.

_____9. Which creates disorder in the institution.

_____10. Officer Link and I talked with both Opeya and Armstrong about appropriate behavior in our workshop.

Chapter 15

Run-on Sentences

Of all the mistakes a writer can make, run-on sentences are among the most serious. So what's a run-on sentence, and how can you avoid making this error?

A "run-on" is two sentences joined together without a period:

The dog barked in the middle of the night, Wilson looked out the window. RUN-ON
The dog barked in the middle of the night. Wilson looked out the window. CORRECT

A fight broke out near the canteen, two inmates were arguing about a chicken sandwich. RUN-ON
A fight broke out near the canteen. Two inmates were arguing about a chicken sandwich. CORRECT

The problem with a run-on is that it doesn't stop when it's supposed to. (Think of a car engine that "runs on": It's the same problem—not stopping when it's supposed to.)

Some officers wrongly think that any long sentence is a "run-on." Not true! Long sentences are perfectly correct *as long as* there's a period in the right place. Here's a long sentence from Thomas Jefferson's first Inaugural Address. It's grammatically correct and doesn't need any corrections:

And let us reflect that, having banished from our land that religious intolerance under which mankind so long bled and suffered, we have yet gained little if we countenance a political intolerance as despotic, as wicked, and capable of as bitter and bloody persecutions. CORRECT

Actually some run-ons are quite short. They're still wrong if the period is missing. (Note, by the way, that some teachers and editors use the term "fused sentence": It's the same thing.)

Jane was frightened, she hid in the closet. RUN-ON
Jane was frightened. She hid in the closet. CORRECT

I pushed, the door opened. RUN-ON
I pushed. The door opened. CORRECT

Avoiding Run-on Sentences

Here are a few suggestions to help you avoid run-ons:

- Remember that "it" often starts a new sentence:

   I searched his locker, it was empty. RUN-ON
   I searched his locker. It was empty. CORRECT

- Practice distinguishing between "extra ideas" (which end in commas) and sentences (which require periods or semicolons):

   When the alarm went off, we ran to the back door. CORRECT ("When the alarm went off" is an extra idea)
   The alarm went off, we ran to the back door. RUN-ON
   The alarm went off. We ran to the back door. CORRECT

- Study pages 99 – 103, which cover semicolons and periods, to gain confidence with punctuation.

Exercise 16 Identifying and Correcting Run-on Sentences

Instructions: Insert periods or semicolons where they're needed. Some sentences don't need corrections. When you're finished, check your answers on page 199.

1. Knudsen saw someone photographing the Rizzo house, no charges were filed.

2. When I entered the sun porch, I saw marijuana plants growing in front of the south window.

3. The emergency room was crowded Duran signed herself out.

4. Culpepper said the suspect had a snake tattoo, gold hoop earrings, and two missing front teeth.

5. Carr insisted that because he was Belle's father, he could discipline her any way he chose.

6. I approached the dog, it growled at me.

7. Nieminen said she heard screeching brakes and a thud, she told her husband to go outside to look.

8. One car had a dented fender, the other was undamaged.

9. No one enjoys working holidays, however in our profession it's often necessary.

10. I talked to the lieutenant, then I went straight to the gym.

Chapter 16

Misplaced Modifiers

The term "misplaced modifier" may sound like English teachers' jargon, but it points to a real-world writing problem you should avoid in your reports. (Another name for this problem is "dangling modifier.")

"Misplaced" means *hanging*, and a "modifier" is a *description*. So a "misplaced modifier" is a description in the wrong place. Most misplaced modifiers are easy to spot because they sound ridiculous. Take a look at these examples:

> Spattered around the room, Jones photographed the blood. MISPLACED MODIFIER
>
> I spotted broken glass searching for evidence. MISPLACED MODIFIER
>
> I saw a bloody knife walking through the bedroom. MISPLACED MODIFIER

Here are the corrected sentences:

> Jones photographed the blood that was spattered around the room. CORRECT
>
> While searching for evidence, I spotted broken glass. CORRECT
>
> Walking through the bedroom, I saw a bloody knife. CORRECT

Sometimes misplaced modifiers are harder to spot. To most people, this sentence probably looks correct on first reading – but it isn't:

> Questioning inmate Kelly, he said his sister had bought the watch for him. MISPLACED MODIFIER

There are two problems with the sentence. First, Kelly didn't do the questioning. Second, the sentence doesn't specify who did.

The omission might create a problem in a disciplinary hearing, when it's important to identify all the parties involved.

Here's the corrected sentence:

> When I questioned inmate Kelly, he said his sister had bought the watch for him. CORRECT

Be careful when you start a sentence with an *-ing* word: Often it will contain a misplaced modifier. If you do start a sentence with an *-ing* word, check to make sure it's clear who did what.

Exercise 17 Misplaced Modifiers

Instructions: Make any corrections that are needed in these sentences. Not all sentences need corrections. When you're finished, go to page 200 to check your answers.

1. Holding the shotgun unsteadily in his right hand, a shot was fired in my direction.

2. We spotted the abandoned vehicle driving down Parker Avenue.

3. After questioning Li, I left my card and asked him to call me if he recalled anything else about the suspect.

4. Scattered around the room we saw parts of the sofa and chair that had been broken off.

5. Officer Pierarski found the little girl hiding behind a rosebush in the back yard.

Chapter 17

Parallelism

Parallelism often becomes an issue when you write a sentence about three or more things or events. More often than not, the sentence will take a wrong turn when you reach the last part.

To see how parallelism works, compare these two versions of the same sentence:

Bonnie had bruises on her left arm, her throat, and she was trembling.
INCORRECT
Bonnie had bruises on her left arm and throat. She was trembling.
CORRECT

Most parallelism problems are easy to fix. Usually you can break a larger sentence into two shorter ones.

Spotting Parallelism Problems

First you need to know how to spot parallelism problems. Here are some suggestions:

- Pay special attention to sentences with three parts
- Remember that the third part is usually the problem
- Try thinking of the sentence as a little poem

Let's try that "little poem" strategy with the previous sentence so you can see how it works:

Bonnie had bruises on

- her left arm

- her throat

- she was trembling

You can quickly see that "she was trembling" doesn't match the other two parts. The easiest solution is to make two sentences, as noted before: *Bonnie had bruises on her left arm and her throat. She was trembling.*

The sentence about Bonnie would work if there were three items that matched "had bruises on":

Bonnie had bruises on

- her left arm

- her throat

- her right cheek

Here's how the corrected sentence would read: *Bonnie had bruises on her left arm, her throat, and her right cheek.*

Let's try another example:

Officer Hines and I arrested, handcuffed, and put the suspect into the patrol car.

To check this sentence for correctness, think of it as a little poem:

Officer Hines and I

- arrested

- handcuffed

- put the suspect into the patrol car.

You can see that all parts match: *arrested, handcuffed, put.* The sentence is correct.

Being careful with parallelism gives you writing a more professional look. It's an important skill for officers to master.

Exercise 18 Parallelism

Instructions: Make any corrections needed in the sentences below. Not all sentences need corrections. Check your answers on page 201.

1. Connors told me she locked the door, turned on the alarm, and a neighbor had the alarm code.

2. Ricky Lopez stole a bicycle, a laptop, and he hid them in the basement of his parents' house.

3. Each applicant must submit a birth certificate, take a physical examination, and come in for an interview.

4. In recent years we've been recruiting more women, minorities, and taking a harder line on racism and sexism.

5. Always check your reports for accuracy, correct spelling, and completeness before you submit them.

Section IV

Professional Sentences

Chapter 18

Writing Effective Sentences

As a criminal justice officer, you'll need to write clear, error-free sentences that sound professional. When you're looking ahead to promotion, effective sentences are even more important.

The problem, of course, is that mastering grammar can be a daunting and time-consuming task. What busy officer has time to grapple with adverbial clauses, correlative conjunctions, and appositives? Suppose, though, that you had to master only four sentence patterns—and (even better) you realized that you already knew the rules for writing them. Now the task is manageable.

We can call them **subordinate conjunction**, **coordinate conjunction**, **semicolon**, and **interrupter** sentences.

Professional Sentence Patterns		
Type of Pattern	**Special Words**	**Typical Sentence**
subordinate conjunction (Comma Rule 1)	**if**, **when**, **because**, **although**, and similar words	Because of the fog, inmates remained in their cells.
coordinate conjunction (Comma Rule 2)	**FANBOYS** words: **for**, **and**, **nor**, **but**, **or**, **yet**, **so**	I suggested an ambulance, but Caffrey refused medical care.
interrupter (Comma Rule 3)	**who**, **which**	Officer Jagger, who joined the force last year, will head the new project.
semicolon	none required	The new law goes into effect today; it will broaden police powers.

A Closer Look

As the chart on page 97 demonstrates, three of the sentence patterns correspond to the three Comma Rules on pages 105 – 116. Semicolon sentences are even easier to learn. Semicolons are like periods: The only difference is that you lower-case the first word after a semicolon.

In the following pages you'll learn the special words and punctuation needed for each type of sentence, and you'll have a chance to practice applying what you've learned.

Chapter 19

Periods and Semicolons

Professional Sentence Patterns		
Type of Pattern	**Special Words**	**Typical Sentence**
subordinate conjunction (Comma Rule 1)	if, when, because, although, and similar words	Because the fog was thick, inmates remained in their cells.
coordinate conjunction (Comma Rule 2)	FANBOYS words: for, and, nor, but, or, yet, so	I suggested an ambulance, but Caffrey refused medical care.
interrupter (Comma Rule 3)	who, which	Officer Jagger, who joined the force last year, will head the new project.
semicolon	**none required**	**The new law goes into effect today; it will broaden police powers.**

For most writers, periods are the easiest punctuation marks. You already know that sentences end with periods, and that most abbreviations are followed by periods (although some organizations no longer use them).

When you're uncertain about an abbreviation, you can check their website or look at their stationery to see whether periods are needed. UNICEF, IBM, and NASA are examples of organizations that do not use periods. Mr., Dr., Sgt., and similar titles do use periods. If you're uncertain, check the dictionary or visit www.Dictionary.com.

Here's one more piece of information about periods that may prove useful: Space once (not twice) after a period when you're typing. Today's computers are sophisticated typography machines, and the old rules about typewriters no longer apply.

Semicolons

Once you know how to use a period at the end of a sentence, you also know how to use a semicolon: Just change a period to a semicolon, and lower-case the next letter (unless it's a name with a capital letter). Please note that what you *don't* do is pick out a long sentence, find the midpoint, and stick a semicolon there.

Note these examples:

Garrett unlocked the door. We entered the house. PERIOD
Garrett unlocked the door; we entered the house. SEMICOLON

Mark tried hiding the car keys. Judy found them anyway and took his car. PERIOD
Mark tried hiding the car keys; Judy found them anyway and took his car. SEMICOLON

Semicolons are easy to use, and they give your reports a professional look that impresses readers. Forget anything you've heard about elaborate rules for using semicolons. All you need to do is find two sentences that seem to go together.

Take a look at these examples:

Patterson walked back to his car. The hood was up, and his battery was gone. CORRECT

Patterson walked back to his car; the hood was up, and his battery was gone. CORRECT

We continued the count. Bradley's cell was empty. CORRECT

We continued the count; Bradley's cell was empty. CORRECT

Using Semicolons Effectively

Here are a few suggestions for using semicolons effectively:

- Use semicolons sparingly: One semicolon per paragraph, or one per page in a short writing task.

- Never use semicolons to divide sentences. A semicolon is like a period, not a comma.

- Think of a semicolon as a way to join two sentences into one big one with one capital letter.

- Remember that semicolons are just like periods. You never have to use a semicolon between two sentences. A period will always work.

- Don't be intimidated by semicolons. Any time you have two sentences that are related in some way (and that's most of the time!) you can change a period to a semicolon.

Semicolon or Comma?

Don't try joining sentences with a comma unless you're using Comma Rule 2 (see page 111): Use a semicolon instead (or a period with a capital letter). Here are a few helpful tips:

1. *It* often starts a new sentence and needs a semicolon (or a period and a capital letter).

I like my new laptop, it makes writing easier. INCORRECT
I like my new laptop; it makes writing easier. CORRECT
I like my new laptop. It makes writing easier. CORRECT

2. *However, then, therefore,* and similar words can't be used with a comma to join sentences. Again, use a semicolon (or a period and a capital letter). Only seven words in the English language can be used

101

with a comma to join sentences: *For, and, nor, but, or, yet, so.* (Go to page 111 to learn more about Comma Rule 2 and these words.)

> Lister ran out of the bank, then he jumped into a red Camry parked at the curb with its engine running. INCORRECT
> Lister ran out of the bank; then he jumped into a red Camry parked at the curb with its engine running. CORRECT
> Lister ran out of the bank. Then he jumped into a red Camry parked at the curb with its engine running. CORRECT

Exercise 19 Using Semicolons

Instructions: Read the paragraphs below. In each paragraph, choose two sentences to combine with a semicolon. Check your semicolon sentences against the Answer Key on page 201.

Luther Shalit is a math tutor in the prison GED program. He helps inmates learn elementary algebra and geometry. I've seen positive changes since he became a tutor. Luther is proud of his knowledge and happy to be doing something useful. Luther has always been interested in mathematics. Before coming to prison he was planning to study bookkeeping.

Captain Gephardt asked Linda Hammond to talk to us. She described her work as a Resource Officer at Penny Lane Middle School. She feels she's making a positive difference there. Discipline at the school has improved since she was assigned there. Students trust her and come to her for advice. She discusses substance abuse, family problems, and conflict resolution with students and faculty.

Exercise 20 More Practice with Semicolons

Instructions: Read the sentences below and insert semicolons (or periods and capital letters) where necessary. Check your sentences against the Answer Key on page 202.

1. Contraband is a big problem, it comes into the institution in various ways.

2. The compound was quiet during the weekend although a few inmates tried to instigate trouble.

3. I'm going to interview Davis this weekend, he may have some information about the missing items.

4. I looked for the fingerprint kit, however it wasn't there.

5. We're looking for issues that might come up in the accreditation review, such as hazardous materials and improper recordkeeping.

6. Our agency is planning a series of events to familiarize youth in the community with our personnel and services.

7. The evaluation was a pleasant surprise, we received an excellent rating in several categories.

8. I found a knife under the living room sofa, Shipton found a hammer in the bathtub.

9. After the vehicle crossed the line the second time, I turned on my flashers.

10. The house is equipped with a silent intrusion alarm, furthermore there are bars on the windows and doors.

Chapter 20

Commas

Three basic rules will cover most of the commas you will use in your reports.

Rule 1

Use a comma whenever a sentence begins with an extra idea.

Because the suspect was armed, I called for a backup.

If the extra idea is at the back, omit the comma:

I called for a backup **because the suspect was armed**.

If the extra idea at the beginning is very short, you may omit the comma:

Last night we solved a series of burglaries.

Rule 2

Use a comma when two sentences are joined by *and* or *but*.

I kicked the door, and I pushed it open.

Wilson remembered the incident, but she didn't recall the date.

If you don't have two complete sentences, omit the comma:

I kicked the door and pushed it open.

Wilson remembered the incident but not the date.

Comma Rule 2 can also be used with five additional words: *for, nor, or, yet, so.* For in this context means "because": *Officer Danson suddenly turned around, for she sensed that someone was approaching.* Most of the time, however, you need to focus only on *and* and *but.*

Rule 3

Use a comma in front and another one in back when a sentence contains an interrupter (a word group that disrupts the sentence flow).

Officer Bolton, **who was my role model**, is retiring next week.

Park Street, **which is closed to traffic today**, will reopen tomorrow.

Our new headquarters, **scheduled to open in March**, will be much more comfortable.

Omit the commas for essential information:

Officers who earned promotions will be honored in the ceremony.

> Tip: Reading the sentence aloud is a big help with Comma Rule 3 commas. You'll hear your voice drop and then go up again. Try it!

Chapter 21

Comma Rule 1

Professional Sentence Patterns		
Type of Pattern	**Special Words**	**Typical Sentence**
subordinate conjunction (Comma Rule 1)	**if, when, because, although, and similar words**	**Because the fog was thick, inmates remained in their cells.**
coordinate conjunction (Comma Rule 2)	FANBOYS words: for, and, nor, but, or, yet, so	I suggested an ambulance, but Caffrey refused medical care.
interrupter (Comma Rule 3)	who, which	Officer Jagger, who joined the force last year, will head the new project.
semicolon	none required	The new law goes into effect today; it will broaden police powers.

Comma Rule 1 covers subordinate clauses (word groups beginning with *subordinate conjunctions* such as **if, when, because, although**) as well as prepositional phrases (word groups beginning with *prepositions* such as **of, in, by, for, with, to**). (Formally these are called "complex sentences.")

Using Comma Rule 1 Effectively

Here are a few suggestions for using Comma Rule 1 effectively:

- Never place a comma after a subordinate conjunction.

The street was closed because, we were getting ready for the parade.
INCORRECT
The street was closed because we were getting ready for the parade.
CORRECT

• Don't confuse extra ideas with sentences.

I'd like to go back to college. **Although, this might not be a good time**.
INCORRECT
I'd like to go back to college **although this might not be a good time**.
CORRECT

• Use a comma if the extra idea is at the front of the sentence (*not* the back).

I saw the driver toss something out the window, **when he spotted me**.
INCORRECT
I saw the driver toss something out the window **when he spotted me**.
CORRECT
When he spotted me, I saw the driver toss something out the window.
CORRECT

Exercise 21 Comma Rule 1

Instructions: Use Comma Rule 1 to insert commas where needed. Not every sentence needs commas. When you're finished, check your answers on page 203.

1. While Officer Josephs called for an ambulance I questioned Donner about the shooting.

2. The fight began when Todman insulted Jeffers.

3. Officer Peters impressed the jury although he was nervous about testifying.

4. Because no shrubbery was broken I knew the burglar didn't jump from an upstairs window.

5. If you talk to Wilson in the bedroom I will interview his wife in the kitchen.

6. He has been incarcerated since January 2004.

7. Because I suspected he had a concealed weapon I called for a backup.

8. We routinely pat down inmates after they've been to the visiting park.

9. When the fight broke out in Baker Dorm Officer Cary radioed for help.

10. Although the surveillance camera wasn't working we found two eyewitnesses who saw the incident.

Chapter 22

Comma Rule 2

Professional Sentence Patterns		
Type of Pattern	**Special Words**	**Typical Sentence**
subordinate conjunction (Comma Rule 1)	if, when, because, although, and similar words	Because the fog was thick, inmates remained in their cells.
coordinate conjunction **(Comma Rule 2)**	**FANBOYS words: for, and, nor, but, or, yet, so**	**I suggested an ambulance, but Caffrey refused medical care.**
relative pronoun (Comma Rule 3)	who, which	Officer Jagger, who joined the force last year, will head the new project.
semicolon	none required	The new law goes into effect today; it will broaden police powers.

Comma Rule 2 covers sentences combined with the words **and** or **but**. (Formally these are called "compound sentences.")

Actually there are seven words for Comma Rule 2: **and/but** are by far the most common. The word FANBOYS is a good memory device to remember all seven Comma Rule 2 words: **For And Nor But Or Yet So**.

"For" has a special meaning in a Comma Rule 2 sentence: It's much like *because*.

We've been expecting you, for Colonel Mays said you'd be visiting us soon. CORRECT

Using Comma Rule 2 Effectively

Here are a few suggestions for using Comma Rule 2:

- Never use a comma directly after a coordinate conjunction.

I was nervous at first but, I soon got over my fears. INCORRECT
I was nervous at first, but I soon got over my fears. CORRECT

- The seven coordinate conjunctions (FANBOYS words) are the only words you can use with a comma to join two sentences. Use periods or semicolons with other words.

Bill examined the lock, **then** he looked at the windows. INCORRECT
Bill examined the lock. **Then** he looked at the windows. CORRECT

The promotion I'm interested in pays well, **therefore,** I expect a lot of competition. INCORRECT
The promotion I'm interested in pays well. **Therefore,** I expect a lot of competition. CORRECT

- *And/But* are the most common Comma Rule 2 words. You'll rarely need to think about the other five FANBOYS words.

Exercise 22 Comma Rule 2

Instructions: The key to Comma Rule 2 is thinking about the words *and* and *but*. Check to see if there's a sentence before and after *and/but*. If that's the case, insert a comma. (Not every sentence needs a comma.) When you're finished, check your answers on page 204.

1. Inmate Greene grabbed the garbage can lid and banged it on the mess hall door.

2. I talked to Jerry Whitman and Officer Barthes questioned his wife.

3. Cashin produced a key but couldn't open the door.

4. The policy makes sense but we can't implement it this year.

5. The bright lights disoriented Jeffords and the loud noise confused him.

6. Myers failed both sobriety tests and I smelled beer on his breath.

7. The shelter is overcrowded and does not provide enough services for domestic violence victims.

8. I got out of my car and called for a backup.

9. We questioned the neighbors but no one heard anything unusual that night.

10. I looked for footprints but didn't see any.

Chapter 23

Comma Rule 3

Professional Sentence Patterns		
Type of Pattern	**Special Words**	**Typical Sentence**
subordinate conjunction (Comma Rule 1)	if, when, because, although, and similar words	Because the fog was thick, inmates remained in their cells.
coordinate conjunction (Comma Rule 2)	FANBOYS words: for, and, nor, but, or, yet, so	I suggested an ambulance, but Caffrey refused medical care.
interrupter **(Comma Rule 3)**	**who, which**	**Officer Jagger, who joined the force last year, will head the new project.**
semicolon	none required	The new law goes into effect today; it will broaden police powers.

Use Comma Rule 3 when a word or group of words interrupts a sentence. In most cases you'll use two commas, and changes in your voice will tell you where the commas go:

Your mission, Jim, is to investigate the escape plot we discovered. CORRECT

Your next assignment, which you'll find challenging, is to chair the accreditation committee. CORRECT

Both inmates, Watson and Turner, are being transferred tomorrow. CORRECT

I spoke to Lily Roberts, the boy's aunt, who told me she'd mentioned her suspicions about him to his parents several times. CORRECT

Using Comma Rule 3 Effectively

Here are a few suggestions for using Comma Rule 3 effectively:

- Listen to your voice. Use the commas when your voice changes.
- Use two commas, not one, in most sentences.
- Remember that often (but not always), Comma Rule 3 sentences include a who or which phrase.

  Mrs. Jones, who told me she'd called 911, said the screams began at approximately 10:30. CORRECT

  Inmate Withers, who works in the staff canteen, said he saw Inmate Brown punch Inmate Coleman in the face. CORRECT

Exercise 23 Comma Rule 3

Instructions: Read each sentence aloud, listening for a voice change. Insert commas where needed. Check your answers against the Answer Key on page 204.

1. Patterson Correctional Institution which opened last month is already overcrowded.

2. Sergeant Rice who teaches in the academy part-time has some good suggestions about preparing for the state certification exam.

3. During the winter when many homeless people migrate to Florida the crime rate increases here.

4. Our new evidence room which opened last month is better organized and more secure.

5. Inmate Gleason's girlfriend who visited him yesterday may have supplied the cocaine.

Exercise 24 Practice with Comma Rules 1, 2, and 3

Instructions: Use all three rules to place commas in these sentences. Not every sentence needs commas. When you're finished, check your answers on page 205.

1. As I approached the house I heard a woman scream.

2. Linda grabbed her son's hand and they ran down the street.

3. Linda grabbed her son's hand and ran down the street.

4. Paul who just graduated from the academy is planning to go back for a degree.

5. I went back to Porter Street because I had more questions for Mrs. Smith.

6. Bailey's uniform which should have been soiled was suspiciously clean.

7. Menzies arrived at the meeting on time although traffic downtown was moving slowly.

8. The sally port closed for repairs this week will reopen on Tuesday.

9. Glenn was afraid of weapons at first but soon overcame his fears.

10. He spent extra time on the firing range and asked Officer Kelly to work with him.

Section IV

Mastering English Usage

Chapter 24

Apostrophes

Officers need to know two ways to use apostrophes: in **contractions** (*can't*, *didn't*, *won't*), and in **"of" ideas**: *Mary's uniform* (uniform of Mary), *an inmate's visitors* (visitors of an inmate), *Wednesday's meeting* (meeting of Wednesday).

Apostrophes DO NOT mean "more than one." Note these examples:

Neighbors called the police when they heard gunshots. (no apostrophe)

The Browns live on the next block. (no apostrophe

The Browns' house has a swimming pool.   (apostrophe: house of the Browns)

Karen's statute book is on her desk.   (apostrophe: book of Karen)

There are two Karens in my FTO class. (no apostrophe)

(There's one exception to the "no plurals" rule: Apostrophes are used in the plurals of numerals and letters: *10's and 20's, p's and q's*. You'll learn more about these apostrophes later.)

Where Does the Apostrophe Go?

Before the *s* or after the *s*? It depends on how the word is spelled. Apostrophes always go after the **last letter** of a word or name. If you know how to spell the word or name, you know where the apostrophe goes:

John   **John's** injuries aren't serious.
Louis   **Louis'** car was stolen.

Mr. Brown   Mr. **Brown's** story needs to be checked.
The Browns   The **Browns'** neighbors called 911.

baby   The **baby's** mother disappeared.
babies   We're collecting **babies'** clothing for the charity drive.

family   Officer Clay is investigating the **family's** problems.
families   Both **families'** houses were damaged.

woman   I heard a **woman's** voice on the phone, but I couldn't identify it.
women   **Women's** roles in law enforcement have expanded over the years.

boy   A **boy's** bicycle was found in some shrubbery.
boys   The **boys'** teacher is on paid leave.

Sometimes apostrophes are needed in time expressions:

a **day's** pay (pay of a day)

two **days'** absence (absence of two days)

a good **night's** sleep   (sleep of a good night)

three **years'** experience (experience of three years)

a **week's** vacation   (vacation of a week)

If you don't have an "of" expression or a contraction, don't use an apostrophe:

The **Johnsons** sent me a birthday card.
The **Johnsons'** birthday card surprised me.

My **family's** vacation wasn't long enough.
Having fun together keeps **families** strong.

Contractions

Apostrophes represent omitted letters in contractions: *don't, can't, won't.* Be careful with spelling. For example, in *don't* the apostrophe replaces the missing "o" in *not.*

I am getting ready for my trip to Cleveland.
I'm getting ready for my trip to Cleveland.

Joe is going with me.
Joe's going with me.

Possessive pronouns (like *his*) don't get apostrophes:

That book is **hers**, and this one is **mine**.

Florida is seeing a decline in **its** population.

The Acme Corporation doubled **its** profits last year.

Is that beautiful car **yours**?

It's has only one meaning, a contraction of *it is:*

I won't need a ride home unless **it's** raining.

It's difficult to find a suitable gift for my mother-in-law.

When *its* is possessive (like *his*), omit the apostrophe:

My favorite shirt is missing two of **its** buttons.

Our town got more than **its** share of rain last week.

There's one more way to use apostrophes. When you're writing the plural of a numeral or a letter, use an apostrophe:

Dot your i's and cross your t's.

The cashier gave me my change in 1's and 5's.

During the 60's, many young people protested the Vietnam War.

Exercise 25: Apostrophes

Instructions: Insert apostrophes where needed. Hint: Remember that apostrophes are used in "of" ideas. They don't signify "more than one." When you're finished, check your answers on page 205.

1. The sergeants desk is cluttered with papers.

2. Her stepchildrens claims are unfounded.

3. The puppies were turned over to an animal shelter.

4. The puppies condition is expected to improve.

5. Miss Jones office is down the hall.

6. We all benefited from hearing James explain the new policy.

7. James explanation cleared up several misunderstandings.

8. Families need to understand the special nature of police work.

9. Both FTO instructors did an excellent job.

10. After a weeks vacation, I was ready to return to work.

Exercise 26 More Practice with Apostrophes

Instructions: Insert apostrophes where needed. Not every sentence needs an apostrophe. Check your answers on page 206.

1. I dont understand how to use this fingerprint kit.

2. Once again, the Smiths party got out of control.

3. Two days work was lost when the computer system went down.

4. Lieutenant Conner asked me to address the familys concerns.

5. Last months paychecks will be ready at nine o'clock.

6. I saw scratch marks on the front door of the Browns house.

7. Officer Lewis investigation was thorough and efficient.

8. The Browns were out of town all weekend.

9. A TV in the childrens bedroom is missing.

10. Mrs. Hansens jewelry box was still in its usual place.

Chapter 25

Quotation Marks

On page 59 you learned about quoting victims, witnesses, and suspects accurately. In this chapter you'll learn how to use periods and commas with quotation marks. There are two basic principles to remember:

1. In the United States, periods and commas always go *inside* (before) quotation marks at the end of a sentence. There are no exceptions. (Canada and the United Kingdom use a different system.)

Note these examples:

Linda said, "I checked the nightstand for his revolver. It was gone."

"Put down that knife," I told Wallace.

"When did you come home from work?" Lewis asked.

Lane said, "I'll kill her if she shows her face around here again."

"Stop!" I shouted as the suspect advanced toward me.

2. Use quotation marks only for a person's *exact* words. If you change the words in any way, omit the quotation marks.

Linda said, "I checked the nightstand for his revolver. It was gone." QUOTATION MARKS NEEDED

Linda told me she checked the nightstand for his revolver, but it was gone. NO QUOTATION MARKS

I asked Potter, "Do you know where Brand is living?" QUOTATION MARKS

I asked Potter if he knew where Brand was living. NO QUOTATION MARKS

Exercise 27 Using Quotation Marks

Instructions: Make any corrections that are needed in these sentences. Use the sentences on page 125 as models. (Some sentences are already correct.) When you're finished, check your answers on page 207.

1. Katherine said that "she had never seen the suspect before he attacked her on her front porch."

2. Sarah told me, "I heard someone walking around downstairs and called 911."

3. Brent said, "My credit cards and cash are missing".

4. I asked, did you lock your doors before going to bed?

5. "I asked a neighbor to keep an eye on the house while we were away." Said Barton.

6. "The diamond earrings I kept in that box are missing," said Farrell.

7. Lieutenant Hoffman warned Inmate Rogers, "not to enter the building without a pass."

8. "When will you complete your FTO class?" I asked Susan.

9. Officer West asked Linda Hamilton if she had heard any strange noises coming from next door?

10. Put your hands behind your back I shouted.

Chapter 26

Pronouns

Pronouns are short, everyday words like *I, me, we, us, she, he,* her, *him, they, us, you,* and *it* that we use in place of other words. It would be clumsy to say something like "Mary said that Mary can't come to the meeting." Most of us prefer to say, "Mary said that she can't come to the meeting."

In most sentences it's easy to use pronouns correctly. But there are four pronoun issues that every professional should know. You'll be reviewing them in this chapter.

1. Singular Pronouns

Several commonly used pronouns are always singular: *any   each every   someone   somebody   everyone   everybody   anybody nobody*

> Every officer was on time for the meeting. SINGULAR
>
> Somebody needs to enter these statistics.   SINGULAR
>
> Any inmate is eligible for the program. SINGULAR

Here's where the confusion arises: In everyday conversation we think of these words as plural. Picture *every officer* in your mind, and you'll probably imagine a room full of men and women in uniform. But a closer look at these sentences indicates that these pronouns are singular:

> Every **officer** [not *officers*] **was** [not *were*] on time for the meeting.
>
> Somebody **needs** [not *need*] to enter these statistics.
>
> Any **inmate** [not *inmates*] **is** [not *are*] eligible for the program

Words containing *any, one,* or *body* are singular:

Everyone uses a laptop to write reports. CORRECT
Everybody likes our new headquarters. CORRECT

Use singular words with singular pronouns (*his, her, its*).

Everyone should have his or her reports completed. SINGULAR

Somebody needs to do his or her job better. SINGULAR

Any officer can view his or her evaluation beginning on Monday. SINGULAR

There were many smiles today because every employee is happy about his or her raise. SINGULAR

Many writers dislike "his or her," even though it's correct, and avoid using it. Often you can revise a sentence to avoid "his or her." One strategy is to make the sentence plural. For example, here's a sentence you just read that requires "his or her":

There were many smiles today because every employee is happy about his or her raise.

If you make the sentence plural, you can avoid "his or her":

There were many smiles today because employees are happy about their raises. CORRECT *and* more natural

Sometimes you can avoid "his or her" by substituting "a" or "the":

Each officer will need three copies of his or her time sheet. CORRECT
Each officer will need three copies of the timesheet. CORRECT *and* more natural

2. Its or It's?

Use *its* (no apostrophe) as a possessive word (similar to *his*):

Every department is making adjustments to **its** proposed budget.

My uniform is missing one of its buttons.

Remember that **it's** (with an apostrophe) always means **it is**:

> When the bell rings, **it's** time for inmates to go to their dorms.
>
> Because it's late, I'll make the phone call tomorrow.

3. The "Thumb Rule"

Use the "thumb rule" when a name appears with a personal pronoun: *I, me, she, her, he, him, we, us, they, them.*

Here's how: Make the sentence shorter by covering the *and* phrase with your thumb. Then use your ear to choose the pronoun that sounds right.

> Let Jane and (I, me) help you.
> Let ~~Jane and~~ me help you.
> Let Jane and **me** help you. CORRECT

> Yesterday Jane and (I, me) helped Greg.
> Yesterday ~~Jane and~~ I helped Greg.
> Yesterday Jane and I helped Greg. CORRECT

4. Comparisons

In comparisons, "finish the sentence" by adding an extra word: Your ear will tell you which pronoun is correct. (Go to page 145 to learn more about comparisons.)

> Bill is older than (I, me).
> Bill is older than I [*am*].
> Bill is older than I. CORRECT

> Cheryl works faster than (he, him).
> Cheryl works faster than he [*does*].
> Cheryl works faster than **he**. CORRECT

> Joe speaks Spanish better than (I, me).
> Joe speaks Spanish better than I [*do*].
> Joe speaks Spanish better than I. CORRECT

Carole has been with the agency almost as long as (we, us).
Carole has been with the agency almost as long as we [*have*].
Carole has been with the agency almost as long as **we**. CORRECT

Exercise 28 Pronouns

Instructions: Make corrections in the sentences below. Not every sentence needs corrections. When you're finished, check your answers on page 207.

1. Did everyone complete their requirements for FTO certification?

2. Its obvious that the academy needs to revise its curriculum.

3. Jill has more confidence on the firing range than me.

4. Implementing the new policy is going to be difficult for the captain and I.

5. Everyone on the force has been talking about their upcoming evaluations.

6. Lois replied to this email before she forwarded it to Sergeant Morris and he.

7. Ken understands the procedure better than her.

8. The agency is proud of its' safety record.

9. Someone didn't sign their timesheet for this month.

10. No one knows that part of town better than her.

Chapter 27

Verbs

Verbs are action words (words like *go*, *work*, *help*, and *run*). Most of the time verbs are easy to use correctly. You should be aware, though, of common verb mistakes that can mar your professional image:

- Using *seen* without a helper (*is, are, was, were, has, have, had*):

Caruthers seen him with his sister several times. INCORRECT
Caruthers had seen him with his sister several times. CORRECT
Caruthers saw him with his sister several times. CORRECT

- Using *done* without a helper:

Hossain done time for burglary in Tennessee. INCORRECT
Hossain had done time for burglary in Tennessee. CORRECT
Hossain did time for burglary in Tennessee. CORRECT

- Using *snuck* (considered slang) instead of *sneaked*:

Chan snuck into the closet outside the major's office and stole a box of pens. INCORRECT
Chan sneaked into the closet outside the major's office and stole a box of pens. CORRECT

- Placing the apostrophe in the wrong place in contractions:

Remember that the apostrophe takes the place of a missing letter: For example, *do not* becomes *don't*; *is not* becomes *isn't*; *was not* becomes *wasn't*; *I am* becomes *I'm*.

Officer Farris was'nt on duty yesterday. INCORRECT
Officer Farris wasn't on duty yesterday. CORRECT

I'am thinking about getting a bachelor's degree in criminal justice.
INCORRECT
I'm thinking about getting a bachelor's degree in criminal justice. CORRECT

If you're typing on a computer, the spellchecker or grammar checker may warn you that you've made an error. Always check your reports before you submit them, and–if possible–ask a friend or co-worker to read your reports as well. It's much better to catch and correct errors before a supervisor, newspaper reporter, or attorney sees your report.

Verb Endings

Many people have difficulty with –s and –ed verb endings, especially during conversation. When people talk, they naturally run sounds together, and we tend to omit letters. In most conversations, that's not a problem. But those omitted letters will detract from the professionalism of a report you're writing.

For example, listen to yourself read this sentence aloud:

Bill tried to find the source of the contraband. CORRECT

Chances are you ran the *d* in *tried* together with the *t* in *to*—that's what most people do.

Here's the problem, though: Are you going to remember to *write* that *-ed* ending, since you don't hear or say it? All too often, officers write sentences like this:

Bill try to find the source of the contraband. INCORRECT

Here's another one. Again, listen to yourself read this sentence aloud:

The memo lists the days and times for next month's meetings. CORRECT

132

Chances are you omitted the final "s" in "lists": It's a difficult word to pronounce correctly, especially when you're talking fast. As a result, the sentence may look like this when an officer writes it:

The memo list the days and times for next month's meetings. INCORRECT

A similar problem arises with *supposed to* and *used to*: Many people omit the *–ed* ending.

I use to work every holiday. INCORRECT
I used to work every holiday. CORRECT

We're suppose to receive a raise next month. INCORRECT
We're supposed to receive a raise next month. CORRECT

Wilson use to fix cars before his arrest. INCORRECT
Wilson used to fix cars before his arrest. CORRECT

We're suppose to attend a training session next Tuesday. INCORRECT
We're supposed to attend a training session next Tuesday. CORRECT

Adding Verb Endings

Misspellings often creep in when writers add endings to verbs. You can avoid most errors by following a few simple rules:

1. In general, drop the silent *e* when you add a verb ending that starts with a vowel:

state	hope	care
stating	hoping	caring

2. Keep the silent *e* when you add a verb ending that starts with a consonant:

state	hope	care
statement	hopeful	careless

133

3. When you're adding an ending to a word that ends with *y*, change the *y* to *i* when it is preceded by a consonant.

supply	worry
supplies	worries

4. *Don't* drop the final *y* when you're adding *-ing*.

study	carry
studying	carrying

5. *Don't* drop the final *y* when it's preceded by a vowel.

obey	say
obeying	saying

Exercise 29 Verbs

Instructions: Correct the verb errors in these sentences. Not every sentence needs corrections. When you're finished, go to page 208 to check your answers.

1. We use to write all our reports by hand.

2. Officer Larsen did'nt see the memo about the new pat-down procedure.

3. Pollard said she seen the suspect run through the alley.

4. I snuck Catherine a piece of candy during the meeting.

5. The evidence consist of a button and some fibers that were retrieved from the scene.

6. It's going to take a while for me to get use to the new search warrant forms.

7. Perkins is suppose to be released from jail tomorrow.

8. Inmates from the vocational program done most of the interior work on the new classification building.

9. The call-out sheet list everyone who has a doctor's appointment today.

10. I've been studing so hard for this exam that I'am sure I'll pass with flying colors.

Chapter 28

Subject-Verb Agreement

1. When a sentence begins with *there* or *here*, reverse the sentence to get the verb right.

Here (is, are) your assignment.
THINK: Your assignment **is** here.
Here **is** your assignment. CORRECT

There (go, goes) two fine officers.
THINK: Two fine officers **go** there.
There **go** two fine officers. CORRECT

Here (come, comes) trouble.
THINK: Trouble **comes** here.
Here **comes** trouble. CORRECT

There (seem, seems) to be many possibilities.
THINK: Many possibilities **seem** to be there.
There **seem** to be many possibilities. CORRECT

2. Don't be fooled by numbers. A *unit* of time or measurement is always singular.

Twenty minutes **is** usually sufficient for interviewing an applicant. (unit of time—singular)
Twenty officers **are** taking exams for promotions. (twenty separate officers—plural)

Two suspects **are** waiting to be interviewed. (two separate suspects—plural)
Two days **is** barely enough time to catch up on my sleep during the weekend. (unit of time—singular)

Five feet **is** the average distance between the tables in the mess hall. (unit of measurement—singular)
Five cars **are** parked illegally on Main Street. (five separate cars—plural)

3. In *either/or, neither/nor* sentences, use the words near *or/nor* to choose your verb.

> Neither the inmates **nor the superintendent likes** the new regulations about visitors. CORRECT
> Neither the superintendent **nor the inmates like** the new regulations about visitors. CORRECT
>
> Neither your report **nor the newspaper articles have** the right information. CORRECT
> Neither the newspaper articles **nor your report has** the right information. CORRECT

4. Remember that prepositions (*in, by, for, with, to, of*) introduce phrases that must be crossed out before you choose the verb.

> **One** ~~of the lockers~~ **is** empty. (skip "of the lockers")
>
> **The box** ~~on the top shelf~~ **is** heavy. (skip "on the top shelf")
>
> **The inmates** ~~in Alpha Dorm~~ are getting chest X-rays today. (skip "in Alpha Dorm")

5. Words like *each, every, any, everybody, anybody* are always singular.

> **Each** of the witnesses **is [not are]** telling a different story. (*Each* means *Each one*--singular)
>
> **Every** inmate **has [not have]** a work assignment.
>
> **Everyone** from both departments **was [not were]** here for the meeting. (Look for the singular word "*one*" in "*everyone*")

Notice that *somebody* contains the singular word *body*—and so does *anybody*.

Exercise 30 Subject-Verb Agreement

Instructions: Choose the correct word in each sentence. When you're finished, go to page 209 to check your answers.

1. Twenty minutes (isn't, aren't) long enough to fill out the form correctly.

2. One of the windows (wasn't, weren't) locked.

3. Neither the brakes nor the clutch (seems, seem) to be working properly.

4. Either the fingerprints or the surveillance camera (is, are) like to help us identify the suspect.

5. Advertising for new positions (is, are) going to be posted tomorrow.

6. Departmental policy about interviews (needs, need) to be reviewed by an attorney.

7. Each of the witnesses (is, are) telling us a slightly different story.

8. All of the witnesses (is, are) in agreement on some of the details, however.

9. There (is, are) problems with Praeger's testimony.

10. There (is, are) a good reason why the attorney general has doubts about this case.)

Chapter 29

Capital Letters

Capital letters aren't difficult to use correctly. Most people know about capitalizing personal names, months of the year, days of the week, and place names. A few special rules sometimes cause difficulty, however. This chapter will help you master those rules (they're surprisingly simple, when you think about them) and use capital letters confidently.

Capital letters present special challenges today because texting is so popular. It's easy (and a serious mistake!) to fall into texting practices when you're typing a report. Always capitalize *I* and the names of people and places, and be sure to apply all the rules in this chapter in every job-related writing task.

Capital Letters Made Simple

1. Capitalize words like *North*, *South*, and so on only when they refer to specific parts of a nation: Midwest, Northeast, the South, the Deep South, and so on. Use lower case the rest of the time.

I grew up in the Northeast but moved to the Midwest after I married.

Several burglaries have occurred in the northern sections of town.
CORRECT

2. Capitalize anything that might appear on a sign. Otherwise, use lower case.

My sister is away at college until November.

My sister attends Florida Southern College.

I think you need to go to the hospital.

North Shore Hospital has an excellent reputation.

The shop at the corner of First and Broadway was robbed last night.

After my last class, I often have a snack at Sam's Snack Shop.

3. Capitalize days and months, but not seasons.

Every winter our homeless population decreases as people move to warmer climates.

December usually sees an increase in retail crimes.

Every Tuesday we have a staff meeting.

4. *Always* capitalize languages.

Officer Perez grew up speaking both English and Spanish.

Does anyone here speak Arabic?

5. Don't capitalize other academic subjects unless they're part of the title of a course, and don't capitalize careers.

I enjoyed biology in high school, but I didn't like physics.

During Criminology 101 I became aware of the amazing range of career possibilities in criminal justice.

6. Capitalize words like *Mother, Father, Aunt,* and *Pastor* only when they're used as people's names.

Did you talk to *Mother* about her plans for the weekend?

My mother is proud that I chose a criminal justice career.

We invited Pastor Taylor and Rabbi Levine to the committee meeting about crimes against seniors.

The mayor invited both a rabbi and a priest to give invocations at the ceremony honoring our fallen officers.

Exercise 31 Capital Letters

Instructions: Make corrections where needed in the sentences below. When you're finished, check your answers on page 209.

1. My mother, father, and grandfather proudly attended my graduation from north central police academy two years ago.

2. Although english and science have never been easy for me, I'm thinking of enrolling in college this fall.

3. The professors who teach Criminal Justice courses have an excellent reputation.

4. You'll enjoy taking Policing Theory and Practice I and II with professor Henry.

5. If you're not sure about a career, you should investigate the possibilities in forensics and crime scene investigation.

6. I'm seriously thinking about becoming a Criminologist, and my sister plans to become a Probation Officer.

7. I first became interested in police work when officer Penny Baldwin started an explorers club at my elementary school.

8. We meet weekly during the school year and did special projects in the Summer, when school was out.

9. Although there's a different sponsor now, there's still an explorers club at Tracy elementary school.

10. Many officers received their first introduction to criminal justice through a similar club.

Chapter 30

Comparisons

"Better than," "as good as," "rather than": These kinds of comparisons often appear in police and corrections reports. Good writers know there are some pitfalls to watch for when you're using these and similar words to make comparisons.

First, remember that our English language is often concerned with the numbers *two* and *three*:

- Use *-er* comparisons (*better*, *faster*, *older*, and similar words) when you're comparing **two** people or things. (The word *worse* and phrases beginning with *more* also fall into this category.)
- Use *-est* words when you're comparing **three or more** people or things. (The word *best* and phrases beginning with *most* also fall into this category.)

Officer Morgan is *more* experienced than Officer Brown. CORRECT (comparing two people)

Officer Morgan is the *most* experienced officer on the force. CORRECT (comparing three or more people)

If you'd spent some time riding with Larry and Tom, you'd know that Larry is the better driver. CORRECT (comparing two people)

Larry is the best driver in our agency. CORRECT (comparing three or more people)

Next, be sure to use *than* (not *then*) in comparisons.

I'd rather work on Saturday than Sunday. CORRECT

The coffee from the staff canteen is better than the coffee in the mess hall. CORRECT

Alan is usually more thorough than she. CORRECT

Finally, when you're writing a comparison sentence, pay extra attention to pronouns (*he*, *she*, *I*, *we*, and so on). Take a look at the last example. Many people would (incorrectly) write it this way:

Alan is usually more thorough than **her**. INCORRECT

If you add an extra word ("is," in this sentence), you can hear that **she** is needed:

Alan is usually more thorough than she **is**. CORRECT

Alan is usually more thorough than she. CORRECT

By keeping these pointers in mind, you can handle comparisons effectively every time. (To review using pronouns in comparisons, go to page 129.)

Exercise 32 Comparisons

Instructions: Choose the correct word in each sentence below. When you're finished, check your answers on page 210.

1. I'd rather supervise inmates in the mess hall (than, then) work in a dorm.

2. Margaret is nearly as good at report writing as (he, him).

3. Brock is the (best, better) of the two drivers.

4. Out of all the places I've worked, I like this agency (best, better).

5. Few people face as many risks as (we, us) in law enforcement.

6. Calvin is the (worse, worst) liar on this compound.

7. I'm good at setting up spreadsheets in Excel, and Gary knows almost as much as (I, me).

8. I like outdoor work much more (than, then) sitting in an office cubicle.

9. I tried both interview techniques, and this one is definitely (better, best).

10. Which of the three applicants is (more, most) qualified?

Chapter 31

Prepositions

The grammatical term *prepositions* sounds intimidating to many people. But it doesn't have to be. The simple truth is that you've been using prepositions ever since you learned how to speak...and you've probably used them correctly most of the time. As a serious writer you need to learn only a few usage rules about prepositions.

What are prepositions? They are small, ordinary words that indicate direction or purpose: *in, by, for, with, to, of, on, over, under, beside, near, along*...you can probably think of many more.

Prepositional phrases are small word groups that begin with prepositions: *in the garden, by the sea, for a year, with my sister, to the store*, and so on.

Here are the usage points you need to know:

1. Most of the time prepositional phrases are **extra** parts of sentences. When you're analyzing a sentence, you should usually skip over the prepositional phrase to get to the really important parts.

> A change in city policies are causing headaches for police officers.
> INCORRECT

What is the sentence really about? Answer: A change. "City policies" aren't causing the headaches: The *change* is.

So the sentence needs to be corrected:

> **A change** in city policies **is** causing headaches for police officers.
> CORRECT

(You can learn more by reading about Rule 4 on page 138.)

2. You can use a comma when a sentence begins a prepositional phrase. Note, though, that many good writers omit the comma if the prepositional phrase is short. It's your choice.

> On Tuesdays Chief Strong meets with the mayor. [No comma: *On Tuesdays* is a short prepositional phrase.]

> Under the bed in a box tied with string, I found a Smith-Wesson revolver. [Use a comma: *Under the bed in a box tied with string* is a long prepositional phrase.]

You can learn more about these commas by reading about Comma Rule 1 beginning on page 107.

3. Shorten the sentence and use your ear when a pronoun (*he, she, him, her, I, me*, etc.) follows a preposition.

> I gave the report to her for proofreading. CORRECT [not "to she"]
> I gave the report to Fakir and her before I delivered it to the mayor. CORRECT [not "to Fakir and she "]

> Chief Strong thanked me for my hard work. CORRECT
> Chief Strong thanked Officer Brown and me for my hard work. CORRECT

You can learn more about sentences like these by reading about the "Thumb Rule" on page 129.

4. Use prepositions with precision. Notice the different meanings in these two sentences:

> Officer McCaffrey walked in the room. [He spent time walking around the room.] CORRECT
> Officer McCaffrey walked into the room. [He entered the room.] CORRECT

Exercise 33 Prepositions

Instructions: Correct the errors in the sentences below. Not all sentences contain errors. When you're finished, check your answers on page 211.

1. In a box on the top shelf of a bookcase I found two instructional books about cockfighting.

2. An array of knives, shotguns, and revolvers was displayed on a table in the basement.

3. A decision about criminal charges for the three men are expected by tomorrow morning.

4. For now the new chief is concentrating on getting to know the officers and the challenges they're facing.

5. By the end of next October, we will be ready to discuss the new budget.

6. Under the sofa in the living room, I found a baseball bat.

7. Misuse of prescription drugs by juveniles cause serious behavior problems in the schools in our town.

8. Of all the applicants for the new position, Patricia Cooney seems the most qualified.

9. An assortment of contraband items were found when we shook down inmates in Alpha Dorm.

10. For the most part, juvenile offenders don't seem to understand the seriousness of what they've done.

Chapter 32

Avoiding Common Errors

This chapter is a refresher about usage points that cause problems for many writers. Take a look at these quick, easy-to-understand explanations. In just a few minutes you can clear up some of the most common mistakes found in police and corrections reports.

1. Not ending sentences with a period.

Here's a quick lesson: Extra ideas end with commas. Sentences end with periods.

When McKay asked for a backup, EXTRA IDEA

McKay asked for a backup. SENTENCE

Although I was going off duty, EXTRA IDEA

I was going off duty. SENTENCE

Here's how to put extra ideas and sentences together:

When McKay asked for a backup, Jackson responded. CORRECT

Although I was going off duty, I decided to check on McKay. CORRECT

2. Not knowing what a sentence is.

Here's a quick lesson: A sentence begins with a person, place, or thing.

He ran out the door. SENTENCE

After he ran out the door, EXTRA IDEA

After he ran out the door, Clara called 911. CORRECT

It's a sentence even if it's short or unclear:

I understand. SENTENCE

He did. SENTENCE

It is here. SENTENCE

Go to page 99 for more help with periods, and to page 105 for more help with commas.

3. Using a comma instead of a period to start a new sentence with *it*. Good writers use a period to start a new sentence.

The rope broke, it wasn't strong enough. INCORRECT
The rope broke. It wasn't strong enough. CORRECT

I rejected her explanation, it didn't make sense. INCORRECT
I rejected her explanation. It didn't make sense. CORRECT

4. Getting pronouns mixed up (*I/me, he/him, she/her, we/us, they/them*).

Jim and me searched the neighborhood. INCORRECT (Think: **I** searched the neighborhood.)
Jim and **I** searched the neighborhood. CORRECT

The captain gave Cynthia and I a special assignment. INCORRECT (Think: The captain gave **me** a special assignment.)
The captain gave Cynthia and **me** a special assignment. CORRECT

For more help with these pronouns, go to page 129 and read about the Thumb Rule.

5. Using unnecessary apostrophes with the letter "s."

Here's a quick lesson: Use apostrophes only in contractions (*don't, can't*) and "of" ideas (*Mary's car, Tom's schedule*). Apostrophes aren't decorations, and they don't mean more than one.

The cars will be replaced in two years. (no "of" ideas, and no apostrophes) CORRECT

John's laptop isn't working properly. (laptop of John) CORRECT

The Browns are taking a vacation next month. (no "of" ideas, and no apostrophes)

My uniform doesn't need to be dry cleaned until next week. (*don't* is a contraction) CORRECT

Go to page 121 for a review of apostrophes.

6. Putting a comma after a subordinate or coordinate conjunction.

Sounds intimidating! But actually those conjunctions are words you use every day: *and, but, if, when, because, although*, and so on. Don't put commas after them. (If you need a comma, put it in front.)

I walked around the whole perimeter of the store but, I didn't see or hear anything. INCORRECT
I walked around the whole perimeter of the store, but I didn't see or hear anything. CORRECT
I walked around the whole perimeter of the store but didn't see or hear anything. CORRECT

Be especially careful with *although*. Anything that starts with *although* is an extra idea that has to be attached to a real sentence (and of course you'll never put a comma after *although*):

He insisted on driving his car home. Although, his friends tried to stop him. INCORRECT
He insisted on driving his car home although his friends tried to stop him. CORRECT

For more help with commas, go to page 105.

7. Misspelling *all right* and *a lot*.

All right and *a lot* are always two words. Always. No exceptions. You can check the dictionary to verify this: It will tell you that the common one-word spellings are "nonstandard," meaning that professionals never use them. See also page 173.

> Leon told me he was all right and didn't need medical attention. CORRECT
>
> Denise said she'd heard a lot of yelling coming from the Wrights' apartment. CORRECT

8. Misusing quotation marks.

Use quotation marks *only* for a person's *exact* words. If you change the words, omit the quotation marks. Go to page 59 for more help.

When you use quotation marks, always put commas and periods inside. There are no exceptions in the United States. Go to pages 125-6 for more help.

> Casey said, "I was afraid to spend the night here with him in that condition, so I called my sister." CORRECT
> Casey said she was afraid to spend the night there with him in that condition, so she called her sister. CORRECT

9. Using texting style.

Because texting is so popular, many people have become careless about abbreviations and capital letters. Beware! If you text often, ask someone to check your reports to make sure you haven't slipped into texting style.

> I will call u when i no the location for our September meeting. INCORRECT
> I will call you when I know the location for our September meeting. CORRECT

10. Misusing verbs or forgetting to use "helping verbs" like *is, are, was, were, has, have,* and *had.*

Writing the way you speak can cause huge problems. Be especially careful with commonly misused verbs like *seen, went, did,* and *done.*

My partner and I seen her get into her car. INCORRECT
My partner and I saw her get into her car. CORRECT

After I had went to the parking garage, Thompson changed his story.
INCORRECT
After I had gone to the parking garage, Thompson changed his story.
CORRECT

Wilkes said he done everything by four o'clock. INCORRECT
Wilkes said he did everything by four o'clock. CORRECT
Wilkes said he had done everything by four o'clock. CORRECT

Exercise 34 Avoiding Common Errors

Instructions: Correct any errors in the sentences below. When you're finished, check your answers on page 212.

1. When I seen smoke coming from the engine, I called the fire department.

2. The lock is sticking, it probably needs some graphite.

3. Alot of honey bun's are sold in the canteens because inmates use them for bartering.

4. I don't no the answer to that question but i will find the answer for you.

5. Many people think that crime rates go up every year but, in many places crime rates have gone down.

6. Although I gave the data to Mary Alice was the one who entered it into the database.

157

7. When I questioned Fischer about the batteries', he said, "he didn't know how they got there."

8. Later Alan Jencks, Fischer's supervisor, said "I don't allow any inmates to remove batteries from the shop".

9. We done everything we could to prepare our headquarters for the open house next Saturday.

10. I'm signing up for a Spanish course next month although, French might be more useful in some neighborhoods.

Chapter 33

Myths about Grammar

There's a lot of misinformation about writing out there. Most people, including officers, learned their writing skills in elementary school from teachers who weren't professional writers or editors. Myths that started decades ago continue to cause endless confusion. Let's clear up some of them.

Discard These Writing Myths

1. "A comma takes the place of *and.*"

No, it doesn't. You won't find this made-up rule in any grammar book. Often, in fact, you need a comma with *and*. (Suggestion: Review Comma Rule 2 beginning on page 111.)

What if you have a list of three items—do you use a comma before *and*?

The answer is that it varies (except in journalism, when it must be omitted.) You can do it either way as long as you're consistent—or you can ask what your supervisor prefers. Many writers find that the comma makes sentences easier to read, so they always use it in a series.

> I arrested Perkins, read him his Miranda rights, and put him in the back seat of the patrol car. CORRECT
>
> I arrested Perkins, read him his Miranda rights, and put him in the back seat of the patrol car. ALSO CORRECT

2. *Ain't* ain't in the dictionary."

Yes, it is—and it always has been. (Look it up!) *Ain't* is a word. Admittedly it's slang, but nevertheless it's a real word with a long history. If you're writing down a witness's exact words, and the witness uses *ain't*, go ahead and include it in your report. Otherwise avoid *ain't*: It can damage your professional image.

3. "You can't start a sentence with *but*" (or *and* or *because*).

There's no such rule. (Go to the library and look for it! It doesn't exist.) Good writers start sentences with these words all the time. Pull some books off your bookshelf and see for yourself. Check the newspapers and magazines you read regularly.

4. "Don't use *I* or *you* when you write."

Old-time report-writing teachers used to warn against "I" and "you" because they were worried about objectivity. What we've learned, of course, is that crossing out "I" and writing "this officer" accomplishes...nothing.

Once again, thumb through some books and magazines and see for yourself. You'll find that good writers use "I" and me" all the time. The prohibition applies only when you're writing for an academic publication or something else that's very formal, such as a legal contract. (To learn more, turn to page 64.)

5. "Use a comma with a person's name."

Not true. Use the comma with a name only when you write a Comma

Rule 3 sentence, like this:

> Patricia Gavin, who joined the agency last week, graduated from the academy with high honors. CORRECT

Don't use a comma in other sentences containing a name:

> Patricia Gavin has dreamed of a career in law enforcement since she was ten. CORRECT

(To learn more about Comma Rule 3, turn to page 115.)

6. "Use a comma when you pause."

True professionals use the three comma rules to ensure their sentences are correct. (See page 105.) If you want to pause for emphasis, use an ellipsis (three periods, like this: ...)

> When Chief Corey retired, we surprised him with...a trip to Hawaii. CORRECT

> On a hunch, I opened the door and saw...the little girl who'd been reported as lost. CORRECT

Save these special effects for writing projects away from your law-enforcement job (such as college papers, personal letters, and writing for publication). Avoid trying for special effects when you're writing a report.

Section V

Choosing the Correct Word

Chapter 34

Criminal Justice Terminology

Like other professional fields, criminal justice has its own specialized vocabulary. It's important to know the meanings of these words and to use this vocabulary precisely.

This chapter reviews words every officer should know. (Because of variations in local laws and procedures, exact definitions may be different in your jurisdiction.)

Adult A person 18 years of age or older.

Aggravated assault Usually involves both a weapon and severe injury.

Alcohol A tasteless and odorless substance. You may have difficulty in court if you claim that you smelled alcohol on a suspect's breath. Better phrases are "alcoholic beverage" or "liquor."

Bias crime (also called **hate crime**): *Not* just a crime by a person who is prejudiced toward a particular group. To prosecute a bias (or hate) crime, you must show that hate motivated the crime.

Burglary A break-in without the use of force against a victim. If someone steals, say, a television set from an unoccupied vacation house, the crime is classified as a *burglary*. [See **robbery**.]

Drunkenness A term for situations involving alcoholic beverages that *excludes* driving under the influence. [See **DUI**.]

DUI "Driving under the influence," including both alcohol and drugs.

M.O. An abbreviation for *modus operandi*, a Latin phrase meaning "procedure" or "method of operating."

Oral: Spoken. [See **verbal**.]

Robbery When the suspect uses force to steal, the crime is classified as a *robbery*. [See **burglary**.]

Verbal Using words, written or spoken. Do not confuse with **oral**.

Chapter 35

Words and Expressions to Avoid

Officers often use jargon to save time when speaking and writing: *BOLO* (be on the lookout), *perp* (perpetrator), *DOA* (dead on arrival.) It's natural to want to sound like other officers, but caution is sometimes necessary.

But there are several good reasons why you should avoid certain outdated expressions and jargon in your police and corrections reports: They're not professional, they might confuse outsiders who read your reports, and the jargon habit can be hard to break when you go on to other forms of writing (if you're promoted, for example). For more suggestions, go to page 56.

Abovementioned

Outdated and often unnecessary. Either omit it or replace it with a specific word or name: *Amy Kallen* rather than "the abovementioned suspect."

Ascertained

Another outdated word.

Be specific about how you found the information (especially important for court testimony): *saw, heard, read, took fingerprints,* and so on. Instead of writing "I ascertained that the suspect had climbed through the bedroom window," describe the evidence: pry marks, broken glass, blood, fibers, fingerprints, footprints.

Affirmative

Substitute *yes*.

Approximately

Substitute *about*.

At the present time

This phrase is often unnecessary and can be omitted—or you can substitute *now*.

Baker Acted

Substitute *I started Baker Act proceedings*.

Being that

Substitute *because*.

Contacted

Not specific enough for court. Substitute *met with*, *talked to*, *telephoned*, *emailed*, *questioned*, *wrote*, or a similar word.

Detected

Substitute *saw*, *smelled*, *touched*, *heard*, *uncovered*—whatever you did to get the information.

Endeavor

Substitute *try*.

Expedite

Substitute *hurry* or *speed up*.

If and when

Substitute *if*, which covers both words.

In close proximity to

Substitute *near*.

In reference to

Substitute *about*.

Mirandized

Police jargon. Substitute "I read him his rights from my Miranda card."

Modify

Substitute *change*.

Negative

Substitute *no*.

Numerous

Substitute *many*.

Pertains to

Substitute *is about*.

Policeman

Substitute *police officer* or *law-enforcement officer*.

Prison guard

Correctional officer is the proper term for an officer in a jail or prison.

"Processed the area"

This vague phrase should be replaced with a specific description of what you did: "recovered two cards of fingerprints on the door frame."

Proceeded

Too vague for a report: Did you drive, walk, run, ride a bicycle, ride a Segway? *Proceeded to* can be changed to "entered" or "arrived at."

Render

Substitute *send*.

Residence

Too vague for a report. Be specific: Was it a doublewide mobile home, a house, an apartment, or a condo?

Respective

An old-fashioned word that's almost always unnecessary.

Take cognizance of

Substitute *recognize*.

Advised or Told?

The word *advise* is a prime example of jargon that can create problems. Many officers mistakenly use *advise* as a synonym for *tell*:

Barlow advised me that he'd been at work when the break-in occurred.
INCORRECT
Barlow told me that he'd been at work when the break-in occurred.
CORRECT

This habit is so entrenched in criminal justice that most officers will understand what you mean if you substitute *advise* for *tell* occasionally. But consider what happens if you use *advise* incorrectly in other settings.

For example, suppose you're writing a research paper for college, an article for a professional journal, a press release for a local newspaper, or a supervisory report. The person who reads what you've written is going to be puzzled if you give the impression that advice was given when actually nothing of that sort happened.

Several teachers at Middleton Junior High advised me that they appreciated my presence at the school. INCORRECT (no advice was involved)

I advised the teachers at Middleton Junior High about handling discipline issues. CORRECT (genuine advice)

Lieutenant Cooper advised me that heavy rain was expected. INCORRECT (no advice was involved)

Lieutenant Cooper advised me to avoid Lincoln Boulevard, which floods after a heavy rain. CORRECT (genuine advice)

This example includes both *told* and *advised*:

I *told* Johnson that his driver's license would expire at the end of the month. I *advised* him to make an appointment right away. CORRECT (only the second sentence involves advice)

Exercise 35 Advised or Told?

Instructions: Change *advised* to *told* where necessary. Answers appear on page 212.

1. I advised Inmate Jones that he was assigned to the morning shift.

2. I advised Inmate Jones to improve his negative attitude.

3. I advised Mary Smith to see a doctor about the cuts on her arms.

4. Smith advised me that her ex-boyfriend was responsible for the cuts.

5. Chief Simmons advised us that he would be on vacation the first half of July.

6. Officer Donaldson's doctor advised him to limit his cholesterol intake.

7. I already advised the Assistant Warden about the broken alarm in Baker Dorm.

8. I'm glad I listened to Chief Johnson when he advised me to continue my education right after high school.

9. The chaplain advised us that there would be a special religious service Sunday evening.

10. My guidance counselor in high school advised me to take a keyboarding course.

Chapter 36

More Words to Watch

A/An

When you're thinking about *a/an*, go by the sound, not the spelling. "A uniform" is like "a youthful offender." "A uniform" is not like "an uncle."

> He was wearing a uniform issued by the Red Robin Casino.

> He became an uncle when his sister's daughter was born.

Advice/Advise

Advice is a noun (a thing). *Advise* is an action.

> I often asked Sergeant Jones for advice when I was new to the force.

> I would advise you to get medical attention for those bruises.

Do not use *advise* when you mean *tell*. See page 168.

All ready/Already

All ready means "all prepared." *Already* means "by this time."

> The lunches are all ready and set up in the mess hall.

> We've already been to that apartment building twice.

All right

In the United States, always two words.

A lot

In the United States, always two words.

Between/Among

Use *between* for two people or things, *among* for three or more.

> The hiring committee is trying to decide between two qualified candidates for chief.

> Cooper, Daniels, and Peterson divided the stolen goods among themselves.

Break/Brake

Break means "shatter" or "separate"; *brake* refers to stopping and the pedal in a car.

> I had to break my appointment to talk with the mayor.

> The brake pedal doesn't feel right.

Breath/Breathe

Breath is a noun (a thing). *Breathe* is an action.

> I smelled an alcoholic beverage on his breath.

> The medic asked her to breathe deeply while he listened to her lungs.

Compliment/Complement

Complement refers to completeness or making something complete. *Compliment* means "praise."

> A full complement of officers attended the ceremony.

> I want to compliment you on the way you handled that incident.

Comprise/Compose

Comprise means "include." *Compose* means "made up."

The committee comprised all 15 department heads.

The committee is composed of representatives from every agency.

Curse/Swear

A *curse* is an evil wish; *to curse* is the act of wishing evil upon another. *Swearing* involves calling upon a deity for verification.

"Go to hell!" screamed Phillips.

Davis said, "I swear I never touched her."

Eminent/Imminent

Eminent means "famous" or "respected." *Imminent* means "about to happen."

She is an eminent authority on DNA.

Seeing no imminent danger, I searched the premises.

Imply/Infer

Imply means "to hint." *Infer* means "to deduce."

Landers said she struck her husband because he implied she was having an affair.

I inferred that Rogers would be out sick for at least a week.

It's/Its

Its is a possessive word (like *his*) and does not use an apostrophe. *It's* means *it is*. The apostrophe replaces the missing *i*.

Her patrol car is overdue for its oil change.

I have to hurry because it's almost time for our meeting.

Never put an apostrophe after *its*: ~~its'~~.

Go to page 129 to learn more about *it's* and *its*.

Less/Fewer

Use *fewer* when you're comparing things you can count, like "gunshots" or "victims." Use *less* when you're comparing amounts that can't be counted, like "cocaine" or "noise." You should also use *less* in expressions like "less than one."

> We received fewer domestic violence calls this weekend than we were expecting. ["Calls" can be counted.]

> This weekend there was less domestic violence than we were expecting. ["Less domestic violence" can't be counted.]

Lie/Lay

Use *lay* when you place something. Use *lie* (not lay) to refer to resting, sleeping, and napping. (Another way to remember: *Lay* is done to things; *lie* is something you do yourself.)

> Sanders was lying on the sofa, watching a football game, when he heard the intruder.

> Don't lay anything on that desk; it needs to be dusted first.

Lose/Loose

Loose means "not tight." *Lose* means "misplace."

> When he realized he was going to lose the argument, Felder hit his wife.

> Carr was afraid he would lose the money, so he left it in a bureau at home.

More/Most

Use *more* when you compare two things or persons; use *most* to compare three or more.

> Law enforcement officers are more professional today than they were thirty years ago.

> I have more experience with white-collar crimes than Marek has.

> Posner is the most skilled block layer on the compound.

See page 145.

Of/Have

Don't substitute *of* for *have* when you need a helping verb.

> Mattson could of have left through the bedroom window.

Passed/Past

Passed is an action that already happened. *Past* is an adjective referring to a previous time.

> Karen said she passed out after taking a few sips of the cocktail.

> In the past, officers wrote their reports by hand or on a typewriter.

Be careful not to write *pasted* ("glued") when you mean *passed*.

Patients/Patience

Patients are people treated by a healthcare professional. *Patience* is the quality of waiting without complaint.

> Many of Dr. Morrow's patients came to him for mood-altering prescriptions.

> Thorough crime-scene investigations require patience and skill.

Personal/Personnel

Personal means "private" or "intimate." *Personnel* are employees.

> Jackson kept his personal papers in a locked drawer.

> All personnel were asked to stay locked down during the disturbance in the yard.

Principal/Principle

A *principal* is the director of a school; *principal* also an amount of money that has been borrowed or invested, and it's an adjective meaning important. A *principle* is a truth, rule, or law.

> The principal wants to expand the D.A.R.E. program in her school.

> Our principal concern is the possibility of an escape.

> Having high principles and sticking to them is vital to the criminal justice field.

Quiet/Quite

Quiet means "not noisy." *Quite* means "rather" or "very."

> It was two a.m. before the dorm was quiet again.

> The evidence is quite clear.

Saw/Seen

Use *saw* by itself, and use *seen* with a helping verb (*am, is, are, was, were, has, have, had*). Go to page 131 for more help with *saw* and *seen*.

> I saw the suspect before he spotted me.

> We have already seen good results from the new training program.

Stationary/Stationery

Stationary means "not moving." *Stationery* refers to paper products used for correspondence.

I spend 15 minutes on a stationary exercise bicycle every morning.

You can get a copy of the report by submitting a request on official department stationery.

Than/Then

Than is a comparison word; *then* is a time word.

Sometimes a dog's nose is more sensitive than our sophisticated laboratory equipment.

If you're interested in advancement, then you should think about going back to college.

See also page 145.

Their/There/They're

Their refers to ownership by two or more people. *There* is an adverb similar to "here." *They're* is a contraction of "they are."

The burglar took all their jewelry.

Couture saw bloody footprints there and called 911.

There are two witnesses waiting to be interviewed about the incident.

They're all in agreement about what happened.

To/Too/Two

To indicates direction or purpose. *Too* means "excessive" or "also." *Two* is a number.

I'm going to the evidence room to submit fingerprints for analysis.

Chen and Wu said they were too frightened to call police.

Horvat is interested in a criminal career too.

I spent two hours searching the database for information about Kovac's business practices.

Who/Whom

Whom is like "him" (notice the final *m* that they both share). *Who* is like "he."

We're trying to discover who had the combination to the safe. [like he had the combination]

The officer who did this should be commended. [like he did this]

The neighbor whom I talked to gave me a good description of the suspect. [like talked to him]

Your/You're

Your means "belonging to you." *You're* is a contraction of "you are."

I'm impressed with the thoroughness of your report.

When you're finished, the data will go into our annual report.

Exercise 36 Words Often Confused

Instructions: Make any corrections needed in the sentence below. When you're finished, go to page 213 to check your answers.

1. We're assigned to the committee that's drawing up a uniform policy about time off for work-related travel.

2. Not all agency personal travel to meetings and conferences, so its hard to be fair to everyone.

3. Your going to find that wearing an uniform doesn't automatically earn you respect.

4. If its alright with the chief, we'll be replacing alot of the exercise equipment upstairs.

5. Safety should always be our principle concern.

6. If the report is to long, I'll help you find places to cut it, and Mike can help us to.

7. Officer Campbell's master's in psychology is a nice compliment to her undergraduate degree in law enforcement.

8. That car just past me going sixty in a 30 mph zone.

9. The courtroom became quite when Caruso went to the stand to testify.

10. Whom is going to meet with the city council tomorrow?

Chapter 37

Using Plain English

Plain English—ordinary words arranged in straightforward sentences—is a great timesaver. For criminal justice officers, who often face life-threatening emergencies, the ability to communicate clearly and directly can be lifesaving.

Some officers, however, are afraid to use plain English on the job. How can you earn the respect of others with everyday words that everyone knows? Shouldn't you try to show off your knowledge?

The answer is, quite simply, no. You need to impress people with who you are and how you do your job, not with pompous language. This is a universal principle that you can test yourself from your own memory bank. Have you ever known someone who found roundabout, fancy ways to communicate? Were you impressed? Chances are you were simply exasperated.

Now think about people you've had great respect for—family members, other officers, friends, and community leaders. What impressed you? Chances are it was their skill and knowledge. In fact you may recall that their vocabularies and sentence structure were pretty ordinary. What caught your attention was their intelligence or some other quality they had developed.

Now think about the people you will be encountering in your criminal justice career—citizens, inmates, officials, and offenders, as well as their friends and their families. Chances are some will be highly educated and accomplished, while others will not. How important is it for you to communicate clearly?

Now turn your thoughts to the reports you will be writing. There will be lots of them, and they will be time consuming. Do you really want to take the time to write 30 words when 10 or 15 would do the job just as well? Picture yourself preparing for a court appearance by rereading a report you'd written six months earlier. Would you prefer a wordy, complicated report, or one that states the facts in a clear, straightforward way? (See page 56 for more suggestions.)

Writing in plain English has three important advantages for officers. First, you can get your reports finished more efficiently. Second, you're less likely to make grammatical mistakes. Most important, the people you're trying to communicate with are likely to understand you the first time. (How many times have you been frustrated by a sentence you had to read several times before you figured out the meaning?)

Choose the Simplest Word

Here's an excerpt from a report about a traffic stop. After you've read it, see if you can find ways to simplify the words and sentences without sacrificing any important details.

> I proceeded to request Ketcham's license and registration. He provided both forms of documentation upon my request. I proceeded to examine them in order to determine whether or not they were in order. Being that he was tapping his fingers in an agitated manner, I commenced talking with him about his destination to ascertain whether something suspicious was occurring. I ascertained that his mouth was dry because he kept running his tongue around his mouth.

And here's a simplified version of the same paragraph:

> While I ran the checks on Ketcham's license and registration, he tapped his fingers rapidly and ran his tongue around his mouth several times. I asked where he was going.

Two Ways to Simplify

Good writers use two strategies to achieve clear, straightforward sentences. **First**, they make wise word choices. Instead of "commence," you can use *begin*. "Adjacent to" becomes *next to*, and so on. "Approximately" (often shortened to "approx.") can become *about*. Instead of "apprehending" suspects, you can *arrest* them.

The **second** strategy is to eliminate unneeded words altogether. Compare these example pairs, noticing that no meaning is changed or lost when the highlighted words are removed:

three ~~individual~~ members
three members BETTER

green ~~in color~~
green BETTER

their ~~respective~~ homes
their homes BETTER

~~At the present time~~ he is a sergeant.

He is a sergeant. BETTER

She ~~currently~~ works as a dispatcher.
She works as a dispatcher. BETTER

He slowly ~~and surely~~ drove to the empty barn with the stolen money.
He slowly drove to the empty barn with the stolen money. BETTER

The following exercise will help you think about timesaving substitutes for unnecessary words and phrases you hear almost every day. Start listening to yourself and others as you communicate at home and at work. What timesaving changes can you make in your own speaking and writing habits?

Exercise 37 Write Efficiently

Instructions: Write a simpler version of each word or phrase. Reviewing Chapter 35 (pages 167-72) will be helpful. Suggested answers appear on page 214.

utilize	abovementioned
single-click	commence
PIN number	relative to
for the purpose of	initiate
the month of October	in order to
yellow in color	residence
large in size	ascertain
in the event that	numerous
if or when	at the present time
preplan	terminate
pull-down menu	being that
take cognizance of	finalize
lower down	endeavor
scream and yell	by means of
brand new	in close proximity to
this officer	modify
inquire	with reference to
transport	answered in the affirmative
pursue	approximately

Exercise 38 Simplify

Instructions: Rewrite this public notice. Think about what's most important, and put that information first. Omit unnecessary words and information. When you're finished, compare what you've written to the simplified version on page 215.

Chief Anna Brown and Assistant Chief Carl Summers have been looking for opportunities to increase community awareness of services our agency provides to the public. It has been decided to hold a one-day Citizens' Academy on Saturday, November 14, from 9 to 4 in the Community Room. Participants will learn about the department's policies and procedures. There is no charge. Interested citizens should preregister by calling 555-1212 or clicking the appropriate link at our website at www.SmithvillePolice.org.

POST-TEST

Instructions: Every sentence has *at least* one error. Make any corrections needed. When you're finished, check your responses against the Post-Test Answer Key beginning on page 217.

1. Parker tried to intimidate me when I told him I was writing a disciplinary report.

2. I asked Santos what happened, and he said that another customer at the bar had hit him with a beer bottle.

3. Hamisch was observed by this officer leaving the shop through the back door.

4. I seen that he was concealing something under his coat.

5. After looking for footprints, the kitchen floor was checked for broken glass.

6. Davies advised me that her ex-boyfriend had been making threatening phone calls.

7. Chapman was screaming and yelling curse words the whole time while I was pursuing him.

8. We contacted individual residents of the building in there respective apartments.

9. Officer Pilak said, "I'am calling an ambulance and your going to be alright".

10. Head nurse Sherry Nowak said, "She heard two men shouting at each other in the hospital waiting room and called police."

11. When I talked to she and her two children about Palmer's whereabouts they did'nt know where he was.

12. Everyone who attended the ceremony said they were very touched by the chiefs speech.

13. Here's the documents that need to go to Wendy and he in the front office.

14. A robbery occurred at the Thompson's house while they were on there annual trip to a resort in the Bahama's.

15. The abuse was reported to Childrens' Services by a Social Worker at the High School.

16. Misuse of prescription drugs are an increasing problem in the elderly population.

17. Guidelines state that bleach and ammonia, which can be toxic are suppose to be stored in a locked cabinet or closet.

18. I contacted Fellowes for the purpose of issuing an invitation for him to make a presentation at our annual conference.

19. This officer pursued Carlson and upon encountering him; verbally commanded him to cease his attempt to avoid apprehension and arrest.

20. I know their hopeing to return home tonight, however we have to wait until the firefighters tell us its safe to enter the area.

ANSWER KEY

Exercise 1 Why Are Reports Important?
page 15

Answers will vary. Here are some ideas you could have included in your letter:

- Your reports may be read by supervisors, the media, community leaders, and attorneys, who will be forming an opinion about you, based on what you've written.
- Your reports may help investigators uncover the truth about what happened.
- Accurate reports establish that you were properly following procedures.
- Effective reports provide information for statistical reports, help you prepare to testify in court, and may even keep you from having to testify.
- An effective report may help persuade the district attorney to prosecute a crime.
- A report may help investigators who are looking for a pattern of criminal behavior.
- You can improve your writing skills by studying the rules of English usage and asking a friend, relative, or co-worker to review what you've written.

Exercise 2 Rewrite a Paragraph
page 23

Here are some problems you might have noted and corrected:

- Labels like *Victim 1, Victim 2,* and *Witness 1* can be confusing later, especially if you're preparing to testify in court. Use people's names.
- Judgments and opinions ("seemed upset," "intelligent," "probably accurate") do not belong in a police report. Simply delete them.
- The officer mentioned checking the door and windows but didn't state the results. Even if you don't find anything, you should document what you were looking for. Including that information shows that you were following procedures and may be helpful later on, as the investigation develops. Suppose, for example, someone tries later on to manufacture signs of forced entry. Your report will help prove what happened.

191

Exercise 3 Preparing to Write
page 29

1. Dealing with a victim's emotions
    a) is not part of an officer's job
    b) should usually be the first step in an interview CORRECT
    c) should be done only after all the facts are recorded
    d) is rarely necessary

2. "Chain of custody"
    a) refers to transporting a suspect
    b) refers to filing a report
    c) refers to evidence taken at the scene CORRECT
    d) does not need to be recorded in a report

3. Having extra paper and pens in a pocket
    a) may be helpful in an emergency CORRECT
    b) is unprofessional
    c) violates most agency's regulations
    d) may damage an officer's uniform

4. Which of the following does *not* need to be documented in a report?
    a) results of a sobriety test
    b) vehicular damage
    c) point of entry
    d) **the officer's theories about how and why the crime was committed CORRECT**

5. Slang
    a) has no place in a report
    b) **may require a definition if it's unfamiliar   CORRECT**
    c) should be used only if it's grammatical
    d) should be used only if it's easily understood

Exercise 4 Write a Report
page 36

Answers will vary. Here's how the report might be written:

At approximately 1:30 p.m. on [today's date], I [your name] was dispatched to 11 Clover Lane to assist a woman who was lost. When I arrived, I saw Karen Billings (WF, DOB 02/10/1999) standing in her front yard talking to a woman (WF, later identified as Joan Murray DOB 11/23/1932) in a blue bathrobe and bedroom slippers.

Karen told me she had gone outside to mail a letter. She saw Joan Murray walking along the sidewalk, looking anxiously from side to side. She looked lost. Karen asked for her name and address, but Joan didn't respond. She kept talking about wanting to find her canary, Buttermilk.

Karen moved into the neighborhood recently and did not recognize Joan. She called the police.

Joan's husband (Stephen Murray, DOB 5/15/1930) came running down the sidewalk, waving his hands. He told us Joan has Alzheimer's.

I gave Stephen the telephone number for Elder Services and instructed him to install a hook and eye on all doors to prevent Joan from leaving the house again. Stephen escorted Joan to their home at 35 Clover Lane.

Exercise 5 Why Is the Report Necessary?
page 37

The report might be useful if Joan wanders again: Elder Services may want to take action to ensure that Joan is moved to a location where she will be watched more closely.

In addition, if questions arise about how the officer handled the incident, the officer has shown that appropriate steps were taken.

Exercise 6 Four Types of Reports
page 46

a) **Type 3** You stop a fight in the parking lot of a baseball stadium.

b) **Type 1** A citizen reports a stolen boat.

c) **Type 3** The manager of a convenience store says she's caught a 14-year-old boy who stole a six-pack of beer.

d) **Type 1** A woman reports that her wallet was taken from her car while she was visiting a friend in the hospital.

e) **Type 2** A citizen comes home from work and realizes that someone broke into his house and stole his computer. (Presumably you're going to look for the point of entry, take fingerprints, and find out of there are eyewitnesses.)

f) **Type 4** You stop a driver who went through a stop sign without stopping, and the driver fails a sobriety test.

g) **Type 3** A technician in an emergency room is assaulted by a patient.

h) **Type 1** In a correctional institution, you spot something shiny under a shrub near the chow hall; it's a pocket knife half buried in the soil. (If you know who put the knife there and take disciplinary action, it's a Type 4. If you simply report what you saw, it's a Type 1.)

i) **Type 4** During a routine locker check in a correctional institution, you find a small bottle of wine—the size served on airplanes.

j) **Type 3** A driver reports that she just witnessed a head-on collision.

Exercise 7 More Practice with Types of Reports
page 47

(Note: Actual situations may not completely match these examples and may require a slightly different type of report.)

1. **Type 3** You'll need to document how you became involved (you were dispatched), what you did (settle the fight), and the disposition (arrests? ambulance?).

2. **Type 1** (if you simply record what happened) or **Type 2** (if you make an investigation).

3. **Type 1** The incident already happened. You record that you were dispatched (or took the report by phone) and record the information about the issuing girl.

4. **Type 4** You're the person who discovered the offense. Explain how you got

involved (why were you searching?), what you found, how the inmate responded, and the disposition (was the inmate taken to confinement?).

5. **Type 2** You and your partner sort out the stories and decide which party to arrest. If you have to settle additional violence while you're there, this becomes a Type 3 report.

Exercise 8 Objectivity
page 53

Words and phrases that lack objectivity are printed in **bold type**.

1. On the east side of 10th Street I saw a WM in jeans and a red flannel shirt who **was behaving suspiciously**.

2. Albert Johnson **threatened** his wife.

√ 3. I smelled an alcoholic beverage on Carol Johnson's breath. (An alcoholic beverage has a definite odor.)

√ 4. Inmate Palmer approached me with his fists clenched. (You can see clenched fists.)

5. I saw **what might be a weapon** in his left pocket.

√ 6. I saw an irregular bulge in his left pocket. (You can see an irregular bulge.)

√ 7. Overturned bureau drawers were lying on the bedroom floor.

8. When I looked into the back porch, I saw **evidence of a break-in**. (Sometimes perpetrators try to fake a break-in. You can't assume that disorder was created by an intruder.)

9. Inmate Chapman **seemed nervous** when I walked into his cell. (What looks like nervous behavior to one person might seem normal to another observer.)

√ 10. Harmon's hands trembled when I asked him to open his locker.

Exercise 9 Rewrite These Sentences
page 57

1. I ordered Inmate Joseph Curry to empty his pockets.

2. Pate's lips were trembling, and his hands were shaking. I asked him where the sealed cartons in the back seat came from.

3. I told the teenagers their skateboards were damaging the park benches. One girl walked up to me and said, "You're not my mother. I don't have to listen to you." The boy and girl with her applauded and then got back on their skateboards.

4. Johnson told me that a man and woman walked into her store and started arguing. The woman wanted to buy a six-pack of beer, but the man told her she needed to cut back on her drinking.
Johnson said then the woman grabbed a six-pack of Budweiser. In response, the man pushed her against the door of the cooler and took the six-pack away from her.

5. Inmate Rogers screamed, "You bastard! Give it back!" when I found a jar of Nescafe coffee under her pillow and took it with me.

6. I told Cooper he was under arrest, read him his rights from my Miranda card, and placed in the back of my patrol car.

Exercise 10 What Did They Say?
page 60

X 1. Patricia said that her husband was abusive to her. INCORRECT – *abusive* is vague.

√ 2. Mark said that his wife repeatedly criticizing his earning power in front of their guests. When he asked her to stop, she threw a bowl of mashed potatoes at him.

√ 3. Reilly told me that he had been at work when the burglary was committed.

X 4. Jones responded to my accusation with an alibi. INCORRECT – *alibi* is vague.

X 5. Linda was obviously covering up for her husband when she said he'd been home all evening. INCORRECT – *obviously covering up* is a judgment.

√ 6. Hayley said she had been to Walgreen's, Radio Shack, and the First National

Bank that morning.

X 7. Dennis showed signs of dementia when he tried to recount what had happened. INCORRECT – *showed signs of dementia* is an opinion.

√ 8. Dennis spoke slowly, in broken sentences. Several times he repeated himself. Twice there were long pauses while he searched for the word he wanted. Finally he said he'd been watching TV when the doorbell rang.

Exercise 11 Think about OJT
page 65

Answers will vary.

Think about ways you could share what you've learned with new officers.

Exercise 12 Using Bullet Style
page 68

Note: These are suggestions only. Answers may vary.

1. When Patterson entered her bedroom, she noticed the following:
   - dresser drawers were overturned and emptied on the floor
   - the lock on her jewelry box was open
   - the jewelry box was emptied on her bed
   - a gold necklace and a platinum diamond ring were missing

2. After talking to the bartender (WM Tom Tippin, DOB 12/06/1986), I entered a private room in the back and saw:
   - a WM and WF screaming at each other (Clarence Coppin, DOB 4/12/1984 and Susan Coppin, DOB 1/19/1986).
   - a young girl (Ginny Coppin, DOB 9/12/2002) kicking Clarence's legs
   - Clarence was paying no attention to Ginny's kicks
   - a BF server picking up shards of glass from the floor (Doris James, DOB 5/03/1987)

   I heard Susan scream, "Get the hell out of here."

3. Dominguez told me:
   - he ran into McDonald's to use the bathroom
   - he left his wallet on the front seat
   - his friend Galleti was in the passenger seat

- a few minutes later he returned to his car
- both Galleti and the wallet were gone

Exercise 13 Using Active and Passive Voice
page 72

Rewrites for sentences marked X will vary.

X 1. The manager saw Jones running away from the convenience store.

√ 2. Jones was carrying a six-pack of beer and a bottle of white wine.

X 3. I administered three sobriety tests.

√ 4. Patterson was looking in his wallet for his driver's license.

X 5. The defense attorney questioned both witnesses.

√ 6. Finch was having difficulty answering the questions.

√ 7. Chief Clancy and Major Mahoney rewrote the procedure.

X 8. Lieutenant Rodgers rewrote the procedure two years ago.

√ 9. I was hoping to take a week of vacation in late August.

X 10. Linda found the wallet under the driver's seat.

√ 11. The mayor will be attending Lieutenant Cohen's retirement ceremony.

√ 12. Luis is interested in forensics.

X 13. Universities are paying top salaries to scientists in crime labs right now.

√ 14. Three years ago, Luis was working in a low-paying service job.

X 15. His manager told him there wasn't much of a future for him there.

Exercise 14 Exploring Online Resources
page 77

Answers will vary.

Exercise 15 Fragments
page 84

____1. Inmate Armstrong asked to go to sickbay at 9:30 this morning.

____2. Complained of a bad headache and nausea.

____3. Although, five minutes earlier he'd been joking and smiling.

____4. Noticing that he kept glancing at Inmate Opeya.

____5. Who was working next to him.

____6. Officer Link told me Opeya and Armstrong got into a shoving match.

____7. Armstrong wanted to avoid a fight by going to sickbay.

____8. Like other inmates who try to manipulate supervisors.

____9. Which creates disorder in the institution.

____10. Officer Link and I talked with both Opeya and Armstrong about appropriate behavior in our workshop.

Exercise 16 Identifying and Correcting Run-on Sentences
page 86

Sentences in **bold** type have been corrected.

1. **Knudsen saw someone photographing the Rizzo house. No charges were filed.**

2. When I entered the sun porch, I saw marijuana plants growing in front of the south window.

3. **The emergency room was crowded. Duran signed herself out.**

4. Culpepper said the suspect had a snake tattoo, gold hoop earrings, and two missing front teeth.

5. Carr insisted that because he was Belle's father, he could discipline her any way he chose.

6. **I approached the dog. It growled at me.**

7. **Nieminen said she heard screeching brakes and a thud. She told her husband to go outside to look.**

8. **One car had a dented fender. The other was undamaged.**

9. **No one enjoys working holidays. However, in our profession it's often necessary.**

10. **I talked to the lieutenant. Then I went straight to the gym.**

Here are the same sentences with semicolons:

1. **Knudsen saw someone photographing the Rizzo house; no charges were filed.**

3. **The emergency room was crowded; Duran signed herself out.**

6. **I approached the dog; it growled at me.**

7. **Nieminen said she heard screeching brakes and a thud; she told her husband to go outside to look.**

8. **One car had a dented fender; the other was undamaged.**

9. **No one enjoys working holidays; however, in our profession it's often necessary.**

10. **I talked to the lieutenant; then I went straight to the gym.**

Exercise 17 Misplaced Modifiers
page 90

Answers will vary.

1. Holding the shotgun unsteadily in his right hand, he fired a shot in my direction.

200

2. Driving down Parker Avenue, we spotted the abandoned vehicle.

3. After questioning Li, I left my card and asked him to call me if he recalled anything else about the suspect. CORRECT

4. We saw broken-off parts of the sofa and chair scattered around the room.

5. Officer Pierarski found the little girl hiding behind a rosebush in the back yard. CORRECT

Exercise 18 Parallelism
page 93

1. Connors told me she locked the door and turned on the alarm, and a neighbor had the alarm code.

2. Ricky Lopez stole a bicycle and a laptop, and he hid them in the basement of his parents' house.

3. Each applicant must submit a birth certificate, take a physical examination, and come in for an interview. CORRECT

4. In recent years we've been recruiting more women and minorities and taking a harder line on racism and sexism.

5. Always check your reports for accuracy, correct spelling, and completeness before you submit them. CORRECT

Exercise 19 Using Semicolons
page 102

Answers will vary. Here are possible answers:

Luther Shalit is a math tutor in the prison GED program; he helps inmates learn elementary algebra and geometry.

He helps inmates learn elementary algebra and geometry; I've seen positive changes since he became a tutor.

I've seen positive changes since he became a tutor; Luther is proud of his knowledge and happy to be doing something useful.

Luther is proud of his knowledge and happy to be doing something useful; Luther has always been interested in mathematics.

Luther has always been interested in mathematics; before coming to prison he was planning to study bookkeeping.

Captain Gephardt asked Linda Hammond to talk to us; she described her work as a Resource Officer at Penny Lane Middle School.

She described her work as a Resource Officer at Penny Lane Middle School; she feels she's making a positive difference there.

She feels she's making a positive difference there; discipline at the school has improved since she was assigned there.

Discipline at the school has improved since she was assigned there; students trust her and come to her for advice.

Students trust her and come to her for advice; she discusses substance abuse, family problems, and conflict resolution with students and faculty.

Exercise 20 More Practice with Semicolons
page 103

1. Contraband is a big problem. It comes into the institution in various ways.

OR Contraband is a big problem; it comes into the institution in various ways.

2. The compound was quiet during the weekend although a few inmates tried to instigate trouble. CORRECT

3. I'm going to interview Davis this weekend. He may have some information about the missing items.

OR I'm going to interview Davis this weekend; he may have some information about the missing items.

4. I looked for the fingerprint kit. However, it wasn't there.

OR I looked for the fingerprint kit; however, it wasn't there.

5. We're looking for issues that might come up in the accreditation review, such as hazardous materials and improper recordkeeping. CORRECT

6. Our agency is planning a series of events to familiarize youth in the community with our personnel and services. CORRECT

7. The evaluation was a pleasant surprise. We received an excellent rating in several categories. CORRECT

OR The evaluation was a pleasant surprise; we received an excellent rating in several categories.

8. I found a knife under the living room sofa. Shipton found a hammer in the bathtub.

OR I found a knife under the living room sofa; Shipton found a hammer in the bathtub.

9. After the vehicle crossed the line the second time, I turned on my flashers. CORRECT

10. The house is equipped with a silent intrusion alarm. Furthermore, there are bars on the windows and doors.

OR The house is equipped with a silent intrusion alarm; furthermore, there are bars on the windows and doors.

Exercise 21 Comma Rule 1
page 108

1. While Officer Josephs called for an ambulance, I questioned Donner about the shooting.

2. The fight began when Todman insulted Jeffers.

3. Officer Peters impressed the jury although he was nervous about testifying.

4. Because no shrubbery was broken, I knew the burglar didn't jump from an upstairs window.

5. If you talk to Wilson in the bedroom, I will interview his wife in the kitchen.

6. He has been incarcerated since January 2004.

7. Because I suspected he had a concealed weapon, I called for a backup.

8. We routinely pat down inmates after they've been to the visiting park.

9. When the fight broke out in Baker Dorm, Officer Cary radioed for help.

10. Although the surveillance camera wasn't working, we found two eyewitnesses who saw the incident.

Exercise 22 Comma Rule 2
page 112

1. Inmate Greene grabbed the garbage can lid and banged it on the mess hall door.

2. I talked to Jerry Whitman, and Officer Barthes questioned his wife.

3. Cashin produced a key but couldn't open the door.

4. The policy makes sense, but we can't implement it this year.

5. The bright lights disoriented Jeffords, and the loud noise confused him.

6. Myers failed both sobriety tests, and I smelled beer on his breath.

7. The shelter is overcrowded and does not provide enough services for domestic violence victims.

8. I got out of my car and called for a backup.

9. We questioned the neighbors, but no one heard anything unusual that night.

10. I looked for footprints but didn't see any.

Exercise 23 Comma Rule 3
page 116

1. Patterson Correctional Institution, which opened last month, is already overcrowded.

2. Sergeant Rice, who teaches in the academy part-time, has some good

suggestions about preparing for the state certification exam.

3. During the winter, when many homeless people migrate to Florida, the crime rate increases here.

4. Our new evidence room, which is located down the hall, is better organized and more secure.

5. Inmate Gleason's girlfriend, who visited him yesterday, may have supplied the cocaine.

Exercise 24 Practice with Comma Rules 1, 2, and 3
page 117

1. As I approached the house, I heard a woman scream. (1 - comma is needed because the sentence begins with an extra idea)

2. Linda grabbed her son's hand, and they ran down the street. (2 - comma is needed because there are two sentences joined by *and*)

3. Linda grabbed her son's hand and ran down the street. (2 - no comma is needed because there's only one sentence)

4. Paul, who just graduated from the academy, is planning to go back for a degree. (3)

5. I went back to Porter Street because I had more questions for Mrs. Smith. (1 - no comma is needed because the extra idea is at the back)

6. Bailey's uniform, which should have been soiled, was suspiciously clean. (3)

7. Menzies arrived at the meeting on time although traffic downtown was moving slowly. (1 - no comma is needed because the extra idea is at the back)

8. The sally port, closed for repairs this week, will reopen on Tuesday. (3)

9. Glenn was afraid of weapons at first but soon overcame his fears. (2 - no comma is needed because there's only one sentence)

10. He spent extra time on the firing range and asked Officer Kelly to work with him. (2 - no comma is needed because there's only one sentence)

Exercise 25: Apostrophes
page 123

1. The sergeant's desk is cluttered with papers.

2. Her stepchildren's claims are unfounded.

3. The puppies were turned over to an animal shelter.

4. The puppies' condition is expected to improve.

5. Miss Jones' office is down the hall. [*Jones's* is also correct]

6. We all benefited from hearing James explain the new policy.

7. James' explanation cleared up several misunderstandings. [*James's* is also correct]

8. Families need to understand the special nature of police work.

9. Both FTO instructors did an excellent job.

10. After a week's vacation, I was ready to return to work.

Exercise 26 More Practice with Apostrophes
page 124

1. I don't understand how to use this fingerprint kit.

2. Once again, the Smiths' party got out of control.

3. Two days' work was lost when the computer system went down.

4. Lieutenant Conner asked me to address the family's concerns.

5. Last month's paychecks will be ready at nine o'clock.

6. I saw scratch marks on the front door of the Browns' house.

7. Officer Lewis' investigation was thorough and efficient. [*Lewis's* is also correct]

8. The Browns were out of town all weekend.

9. A TV in the children's bedroom is missing.

10. Mrs. Hansen's jewelry box was still in its usual place, undisturbed.

Exercise 27 Using Quotation Marks
page 126

1. Katherine said that she had never seen the suspect before he attacked her on her front porch.

2. Sarah told me, "I heard someone walking around downstairs and called 911." CORRECT

3. Brent said, "My credit cards and cash are missing."

4. I asked, "Did you lock your doors before going to bed?"

5. "I asked a neighbor to keep an eye on the house while we were away," said Barton.

6. "The diamond earrings I kept in that box are missing," said Farrell. CORRECT

7. Lieutenant Hoffman warned Inmate Rogers not to enter the building without a pass.

8. "When will you complete your FTO class?" I asked Susan. CORRECT

9. Officer West asked Linda Hamilton if she had heard any strange noises coming from next door.

10. "Put your hands behind your back!" I shouted.

Exercise 28 Pronouns
page 130

1. Did everyone complete **his or her** requirements for FTO certification?

OR Did all the students complete their requirements for FTO certification?

2. **It's** obvious that the academy needs to revise its curriculum.

3. Jill has more confidence on the firing range than **I**. [*I do*]

4. Implementing the new policy is going to be difficult for the captain and **me**. [*difficult for me*]

5. Everyone on the force has been talking about **his or her** upcoming evaluations.

OR All the officers on the force have been talking about their upcoming evaluations.

6. Lois replied to this email before she forwarded it to Sergeant Morris and **him**. [*forwarded it to him*]

7. Ken understands the procedure better than **she**. [*she does*]

8. The agency is proud of **its** safety record.

9. Someone didn't sign **his or her** timesheet for this month. [*someone is singular*]

10. No one knows that part of town better than **she**. [*she does*]

Exercise 29 Verbs
page 134

Verbs that need corrections are printed in **bold** type.

1. We **used to** write all our reports by hand.

2. Officer Larsen **didn't** see the memo about the new pat-down procedure.

3. Pollard said she **saw** [or **had seen**] the suspect run through the alley.

4. I **sneaked** Catherine a piece of candy during the meeting.

5. The evidence **consists** of a button and some fibers that were retrieved from the scene.

6. It's going to take a while for me to get **used** to the new search warrant forms.

7. Perkins is **supposed** to be released from jail tomorrow.

8. Inmates from the vocational program **did** [or **have done**] most of the interior work on the new classification building.

9. The call-out sheet **lists** everyone who has a doctor's appointment today.

10. I've been **studying** so hard for this exam that **I'm** sure I'll pass with flying colors.

Exercise 30 Subject-Verb Agreement
page 139

Answers are in **bold** type; key words that help you find the correct answers are in *italics*.

1. Twenty minutes (**isn't**, aren't) long enough to fill out the form correctly.

2. *One* of the windows (**wasn't**, weren't) locked.

3. Neither the brakes nor *the clutch* (**seems**, seem) to be working properly.

4. Either the fingerprints or *the surveillance camera* (**is**, are) like to help us identify the suspect.

5. *Advertising* for new positions (**is**, are) going to be posted tomorrow.

6. *Departmental policy* about interviews (**needs**, need) to be reviewed by an attorney.

7. *Each* of the witnesses (**is**, are) telling us a slightly different story.

8. *All* of the witnesses (is, **are**) in agreement on some of the details, however.

9. There (is, **are**) *problems* with Praeger's testimony.

10. There (**is**, are) *a good reason* why the attorney general has doubts about this case.)

Exercise 31 Capital Letters
page 143

ANSWER KEY

Words that need to be changed to capital letters are in **bold** type.

1. My mother, father, and grandfather proudly attended my graduation from **North Central Police Academy** two years ago.

2. Although **English** and science have never been easy for me, I'm thinking of enrolling in college this fall.

3. The professors who teach **criminal justice** courses have an excellent reputation.

4. You'll enjoy taking Policing Theory and Practice I and II with **Professor** Henry.

5. If you're not sure about a career, you should investigate the possibilities in forensic science and crime scene investigation. CORRECT

6. I'm seriously thinking about becoming a **criminologist**, and my sister plans to become a **probation officer**.

7. I first became interested in police work when **Officer** Penny Baldwin started an explorers club at my elementary school.

8. We meet weekly during the school year and did special projects in the **summer**, when school was out.

9. Although there's a different sponsor now, there's still an **Explorers Club** At Tracy **Elementary School**.

10. Many officers received their first introduction to criminal justice through a similar club. CORRECT

Exercise 32 Comparisons
page 146

Correct answers are in **bold** type.

1. I'd rather supervise inmates in the mess hall (**than**, then) work in a dorm.

2. Margaret is nearly as good at report writing as (**he**, him). [*he is*]

3. Brock is the **better** of the two drivers.

4. Out of all the places I've worked, I like this agency **best.**

5. Few people face as many risks as (**we**, us) in law enforcement.

6. Calvin is the (worse, **worst**) liar on this compound.

7. I'm good at setting up spreadsheets in Excel, and Gary knows almost as much as (**I**, me).

8. I like outdoor work much more (**than**, then) sitting in an office cubicle.

9. I tried both interview techniques, and this one is definitely (**better**, best).

10. Which of the three applicants is (more, **most**) qualified?

Exercise 33 Prepositions
page 151

1. In a box on the top shelf of a **bookcase**, I found two instructional books about cockfighting.

2. An array of knives, shotguns, and revolvers was displayed on a table in the basement. CORRECT

3. A decision about criminal charges for the three men **is** expected by tomorrow morning.

4. For now the new chief is concentrating on getting to know the officers and the challenges they're facing. CORRECT (Or you may put a comma after "now")

5. By the end of next October, we will be ready to discuss the new budget.

6. Under the sofa in the living **room,** I found a baseball bat.

7. Misuse of prescription drugs by juveniles **causes** serious behavior problems in the schools in our town.

8. Of all the applicants for the new **position,** Patricia Cooney seems the most qualified.

9. An assortment of contraband items **was** found when we shook down inmates in Alpha Dorm.

10. For the most **part,** juvenile offenders don't seem to understand the seriousness of what they've done. (Or you may omit the comma)

Exercise 34 Avoiding Common Errors
page 157

1. When I **saw** smoke coming from the engine, I called the fire department.

2. The lock is sticking**. It** probably needs some graphite.

3. **A lot** of honey buns are sold in the canteens because inmates use them for bartering.

4. I don't k**now** the answer to that **question,** but **I** will find the answer for you.

5. Many people think that crime rates go up every year, **but** in many places crime rates have gone down.

6. Although I gave the data to **Mary,** Alice was the one who entered it into the database.

7. When I questioned Fischer about the **batteries,** he said **he** didn't know how they got **there.**

OR: When I questioned Fischer about the **batteries,** he said, **"I** don't know how they got there."

8. Later Alan Jencks, Fischer's supervisor, **said,** "I don't allow any inmates to remove batteries from the **shop."**

9. We **did** everything we could to prepare our headquarters for the open house next Saturday.

10. I'm signing up for a Spanish course next month **although** French might be more useful in some neighborhoods.

Exercise 35 Advised or Told?
page 171

1. I **told** Inmate Jones that he was assigned to the morning shift.

2. I **advised** Inmate Jones to improve his negative attitude. (giving advice)

3. I **advised** Mary Smith to see a doctor about the cuts on her arms. (giving advice)

4. Smith **told** me that her ex-boyfriend was responsible for the cuts.

5. Chief Simmons **told** us that he would be on vacation the first half of July.

6. Officer Donaldson's doctor **advised** him to limit his cholesterol intake. (giving advice)

7. I already **told** the Assistant Warden about the broken alarm in Baker Dorm.

8. I'm glad I listened to Chief Johnson when he **advised** me to continue my education right after high school. (giving advice)

9. The Chaplain **told** us that there would be a special religious service Sunday evening.

10. My guidance counselor in high school **advised** me to take a keyboarding course. (giving advice)

Exercise 36 Words Often Confused
page 180

1. We're assigned to the committee that's drawing up a uniform policy about time off for work-related travel. CORRECT

2. Not all agency **personnel** travel to meetings and conferences, so **it's** hard to be fair to everyone.

3. Your going to find that wearing **a** uniform doesn't automatically earn you respect.

4. If **it's all right** with the chief, we'll be replacing **a lot** of the exercise equipment upstairs.

5. Safety should always be our **principal** concern.

6. If the report is **too** long, I'll help you find places to cut it, and Mike can help us **too**.

7. Officer Campbell's master's in psychology is a nice **complement** to her undergraduate degree in law enforcement.

8. That car just **passed** me going sixty in a 30 mph zone.

9. The courtroom became **quiet** when Caruso went to the stand to testify.

10. **Who** is going to meet with the city council tomorrow?

Exercise 37 Write Efficiently
page 186

utilize *use*

single-click *click*

PIN number *PIN*

for the purpose of *for*

the month of October *October*

yellow in color *yellow*

large in size *large*

in the event that *if*

if or when *if*

preplan *plan*

pull-down menu *menu*

take cognizance of *learn, discover, know*

lower down *lower*

scream and yell *scream (or yell)*

brand new *new*

this officer *I*

inquire *ask*

transport *drive*

pursue *chase*

abovementioned *above (or repeat the word or name)*

commence *begin*

relative to *about*

initiate *begin*

in order to *to*

residence *home, house, condo, apartment*

ascertain *discover, find out*

numerous *many*

at the present time *now (or omit)*

being that *because*

finalize *end*

endeavor *try*

by means of *by*

in close proximity to *near*

modify *change*

with reference to *about*

terminate *end, finish*

affirmative *yes, nodded*

approximately *about*

Exercise 38 Simplify
page 187

Answers will vary. Here is one simplified version:

You're invited to a free Citizens' Academy on Saturday, November 14, from 9 a.m. to 4 p.m. in our Community Room. Here's your chance to learn firsthand how our agency works. You can register by calling 555-1212 or visiting www.SmithvillePolice.org.

POST-TEST ANSWER KEY

Some answers may vary.

1. Rewrite the sentence to state exactly what Parker said: "tried to intimidate me" is too vague.

2. [Wordy: You don't need to repeat your question to Santos.] Suggested answer: "Santos said that another customer at the bar had hit him with a beer bottle."

3. I saw Hamisch leaving the shop through the back door.

4. I saw that he was concealing something under his coat.

5. [Misplaced modifier, page 89; also you should state whether you found footprints and broken glass] I looked for footprints but didn't find any. I found broken glass on the kitchen floor.

6. [Use *advise* only when giving advice. It would be better to write down exactly what the ex-boyfriend said, and to find out how many phone calls he made to her.] Davies told me that her ex-boyfriend had been making threatening phone calls.

7. State exactly what Chapman said. "Screaming and yelling" is repetitious: Use one or the other, not both

8. [*Contacted* is vague: Did you phone, visit, or send emails?] We **telephoned** ~~individual~~ residents of the building in **their** ~~respective~~ apartments.

9. [Comma Rule 2, page 111.] Officer Pilak said, "**I'm** calling an **ambulance,** and **you're** going to be **all right."**

10. Head nurse Sherry Nowak said, "**I** heard two men shouting at each other in the hospital waiting room and called police."

11. [Comma Rule 1, page 107.] When I talked to **her** and her two children about Palmer's whereabouts, they **didn't** know where he was.

12. [*Everyone* is singular, page 127.] **All** who attended the ceremony said they were very touched by the **chief's** speech.

13. [Subject-verb agreement rule 4, page 138; "thumb rule," page 129.] **Here are** the documents that need to go to Wendy and **him** in the front office.

14. A **burglary** occurred at the **Thompsons'** house while they were on **their** annual trip to a resort in the **Bahamas**.

15. The abuse was reported to **Children's** Services by a **social worker** at the **high school**.

16. [Subject-verb agreement rule 1, page 137.] Misuse of prescription drugs **is** an increasing problem in the elderly population.

17. [Comma Rule 3, page 115] Guidelines state that bleach and ammonia, which can be **toxic,** are **supposed to** be stored in a locked cabinet or closet.

18. I called Fellowes to invite him to speak at our annual conference.

19. I chased Carlson on foot and told him to stop.

20. I know **they're hoping** to return home **tonight. However,** we have to wait until the firefighters tell us **it's** safe to enter the area.

INDEX

About Jean Reynolds

Dr. Jean Reynolds is Professor Emeritus at Polk State College in Winter Haven, Florida, where she taught English for over 30 years. She is the author of seven books, including two writing textbooks, and she is co-author (with the late Mary Mariani) of *Police Talk* (Pearson).

She has taught basic education to inmates and served as a consultant on communications and problem-solving skills to staff in Florida's Department of Corrections. At Polk State College she has taught report writing classes for recruits and advanced report writing and FTO classes for police and correctional officers.

Jean Reynolds holds a doctorate in English from the University of South Florida and is an internationally recognized Shaw scholar. She is the author of *Pygmalion's Wordplay: The Postmodern Shaw*, published by the University Press of Florida.

She is an accomplished ballroom dancer. She and her husband, garden writer Charles J. Reynolds, live in Florida, where they enjoy reading and traveling.

For more writing practice and updated information about report writing, visit **www.YourPoliceWrite.com**. Instructors can obtain a free Instructor's Manual by sending an email from an official account to **jreynoldswrite@aol.com**.